CW01624794

Marc Wal

Strength Through Crises

29/1/25

Marc Wallert

STRENGTH THROUGH CRISES

The Art of Not Losing Your Head

Econ

MIX
Paper | Supporting responsible forestry
FSC® C083411

Econ is a publishing affiliate
of the Ullstein Buchverlage GmbH

ISBN: 978-3-430-21110-9

© Ullstein Buchverlage GmbH, Berlin 2023
Translated from German by
Annette Charpentier
All rights reserved
Typeset using Aldus Nova
Typeset by LVD GmbH, Berlin
Printed and bound by CPI Books GmbH, Leck
Printed in the EU

CONTENTS

INSIGHTS

Dear Reader,

Maybe at this very moment you are trying to find inspiration for dealing with a crisis in your life. And maybe knowing how I survived being kidnapped will be useful. It happened more than twenty years ago …

Until now, I didn't find it easy to talk about it. In the year 2000, the abduction of my parents, me, and eighteen other hostages hit the world headlines. To be the focus of attention after our release was quite a challenge for me, and I consciously pulled away from the public spotlight. I didn't want to feed any more sensationalism, didn't want to tell my story over and over again. But now, twenty years later, I've written this book and give talks about that time, because I've recognized how important it was for me on a very personal level. Maybe reading about it will be helpful for other people too. It's not about the bare facts of my abduction, the "story," but to let others know what I learned from it. Twenty years ago, I was given a second chance. When I returned to freedom, I was allowed a new start and to create a future for myself, just as I wanted it to be. Have I made use of this opportunity? Well, I think so—by and by. But the path to this point has been quite bumpy.

It still amazes me that I survived the kidnapping itself and the one hundred forty days of captivity in the jungle without any damage. It surprised everyone, especially the people closest to me. If I had withstood such an extreme experience, I thought, then nothing in everyday life could ever worry me again. Most people who heard about my ordeal thought the same. But they were all wrong. Five years after regaining my freedom, I suffered a total burnout due to stress at work.

You survived a kidnapping and a long period of captivity without any harm but suffered a burnout at work? Trying to rationalize this conundrum, I began an intensive search for the underlying reasons and arrived at an astonishing insight: my capacity to keep my head played an important part in both crises. In the jungle, it didn't seem to be a problem. But in everyday life, I needed to learn what it takes not to lose it even after a crisis had passed. Both experiences helped me to lead a happier life—and this is what I would like to share with you.

In a crisis, people tend to get overwhelmed by their feelings—mostly by fear, but sometimes by an exaggerated optimism. They are equally dangerous. This is one of the lessons I learned during my captivity. Positive thinking in the jungle could actually be lethal. But this also applies to the "business jungle" of the corporate world. I learned that lesson during more than fifteen years of working as a consultant and senior manager for major companies. In the business world, particularly in these fast-moving times of increasing digitalization, great anxiety prevails.

The ability to keep your head helps you find a clear path through times of uncertainty and crisis. It helped me to survive my abduction and captivity. In this book, I want to describe that capacity—it's almost an art—as well as further survival strategies and how to apply them to your day-to-day life. We jungle hostages developed successful strategies to meet our challenges as a team, and I want to apply those mainly to the world of work.

After they have overcome a crisis, people are often at risk of losing their mind. The presumed comfort zone turns out to be dangerous. "Wow, I made it!" they say. This is a thoroughly human reaction, but it can turn into a problem—unless you simply get back in the saddle again and move on. But you might stumble at the same point again. For years, I made that mistake and ended up on a carousel of crises revolving around the same issues time and again: burnout and broken relationships.

It is quite a challenge to deal positively with the punches life throws. Some blows are so hard that they nearly knock you out. There is no secret formula for how to deal with dangerous situations. During my captivity, when my life was in actual danger, I found consolation in gallows humor. It didn't solve the problems as such, but it reduced the tension. I intend to use humor in this book as well.

Strength Through Crises: The Art of Not Losing Your Head is meant to be a guide about how to be creative and find inspiration—but it doesn't try to be all-inclusive or complete. It's rather about giving suggestions for everyday life. People and their crises are unique, and general advice might not be specific enough. However, examples from my time in captivity, as well as from my personal and work life, might inspire you to master your own challenges and to grow through them.

STRONG IN A CRISIS

Many people have asked me: "How did you survive your dangerous crisis so well? What made you so strong?" Naturally, I've asked myself the same questions. As I sought answers, I discovered some elements of my success that correspond with what I call protective factors of resilience. There are many definitions of resilience—mental resistance, one's inner strength under duress, and so on. Sometimes it is due to seven, eight, or even ten protective factors, also called pillars of resilience. They protected me, and that's why I call them protective factors.

According to scientific studies, resilience most commonly depends on acceptance, optimism, self-efficacy, and social support. Competence in stressful situations and fitness are important too. The first part of this book is a discussion of the six protective factors that helped me most to survive my captivity in the jungle.

Why Me?

That's a question I've asked myself countless times when looking back at my life. I was the youngest in my year at school, physically awkward and intellectually overwhelmed. I would have loved to remain a child, to just play and live without any pressure, staying forever in my comfort zone. During swimming lessons, I stayed in the warm baby pool as long as I could while my contemporaries were already racing each other in the big, cold pool. They practically had to throw me in. I was never a member of one of the cool gangs, and for a long time, I played the unloved role of the class clown.

When I was fifteen years old, things got better. My first love was a popular girl who was definitely out of my league. We spent a wonderful year together and were already dreaming of having children. But it was puppy love, and jealousy and hurt replaced the romance. We separated with tears and heartache. The pain and jealousy nearly tore me apart, but at the same time, those feelings released an unexpected energy in me and made me more courageous. I suddenly wanted to change and at last leave behind my role as the straggler and the clown.

It meant leaving everything familiar behind, and that

was something completely new to me. The decisive moment—and I clearly remember it—came when our English teacher stormed into our geography class and shouted: "Who wants to go on a student exchange to England for four weeks? There are only two places. First come, first served." I had never raised my arm so quickly, shouting "Ja!" *This is my chance, things can't get any worse,* said an inner voice. Another voice reminded me that my knowledge of the English language was pretty poor. But it was too late to worry about that. I was one of only a few students in my class who had never been abroad. My older brother had already been to France and England. He was much bolder and independent and quite a good role model; whereas I was afraid of being far away from home and preferred to stay in the warm nest with my loving parents. But being lovesick worked like a kick in the butt. It threw me out of my comfort zone and gave me the momentum to embark on an adventure—something I had never dared before. For the first time, I jumped into the big, cold pool voluntarily.

The Beginnings of a Self-Determined Life

In Cornwall, I was born again. Laurence, my exchange partner, was a stroke of luck in every respect. I had a wonderful time with him, his family, and his friends. English people seemed to be more relaxed than Germans.

Everything seemed easy, and even learning the language was fun. I progressed in leaps and bounds and conquered obstacles that previously seemed insurmountable. I did a week's internship with a local paper. At the end of it, they published an article about me with a photo. I was so proud! For the first time in my life, I had thrown myself into the unknown and come out the other side! My self-confidence grew amazingly, and I knew I wanted more of that! Back in Germany, I applied myself even harder. I studied, got good grades, found acceptance and respect, and was keen on more—more learning, even better grades. Most of all, I was keen for more recognition. My time abroad had set a positive cycle in motion. But without realizing it, I fell into another trap: I became a junkie hooked on success.

Recognition from others increased my confidence and also raised my status in school. When I was younger, I was quite a talented drummer and had always hoped to use that talent to gain the acceptance of the other students. When I was nine years old, I played for the first time on a large stage in front of an audience of five hundred. It was with the teacher's band, with my father on guitar. At twelve, I won a few talent competitions with the school band. Our songs were even played on the radio (once!), but all that left no impression on my fellow students. The answer to the question "Do I feel successful?" was always no. It would never have occurred to me then that one day I would shine because of my grades *and* be proud of it. But that was exactly the case now. I passed my exams with excellent grades and enjoyed the respect it brought me, having longed for it for such a long time. It felt as if the world was my oyster. In my 1992 high school yearbook, I stated "Abroad (Australia)" as my dream destination.

For the duration of my civil service, I stayed in my hometown of Göttingen to save up for college. I had earned a fair bit of money as the drummer in a band, playing at weddings and office parties for a few years. It had been great fun too.

At nineteen, I had no idea what to do with the rest of my life. Yes, I wanted to go to college and get good grades, and possibly to do it abroad—to hopefully repeat my good times in Cornwall. And that's how my five years in college turned out. I studied all sorts of things—social sciences, economic geography, and international management—in five countries, at four universities, and in three languages. I was ambitious and finished everything with excellent grades. I received a first in my diploma; a distinction in my MSc, and was "Best in Year" as I got my MBA. I was very proud and enjoyed the amount of recognition and respect these honors brought me. Prince Charles would have handed me my certificate if I had gone to the graduation ceremony. In Paris, I was asked to give an official speech as Best in Year in a splendid ministerial building.

My years of studying were exciting and interesting but didn't help much toward finding the right job. I had allowed myself to be influenced too easily, by adverts, articles, recommendations, that kind of thing. I was interested a little in a lot of things (though not in finance), but not really keen on anything, apart from languages. Whereas everyone else seemed to have chosen their favorite subject and committed to it, I was a specialist in the general. I had many fingers in many pies but couldn't decide which one to eat.

"Hey, go into consulting. They are always looking for flexible, well-educated people," a friend of mine suggested. "You can always specialize in something later." That sounded ideal and didn't commit me to anything—quite my thing. Because our careers officer had good connections to Luxembourg, I completed my second master's degree with a corporate consultancy company, Pricewaterhouse Coopers Consulting (PwC) in Luxembourg.

When All Doors Are Open ...

PwC was the ideal springboard for my career. Not only was I part of one of the most renowned management consultancy firms in the world, but also, I was in a heaven of multiculturalism. Consultants from all over the world made up the teams for specific projects. The working language fluidly changed between English, French, and German, often in the same sentence. For me, it was a dream!

For a year, I played the role of a firefighter on a project worth billions, coordinating IT projects for an international financing service. My team of consultants often worked until late at night on factsheets and presentations to finish the monthly report for the board in time. I was a good soldier, but had very little conviction. What I loved was the recognition it brought me.

At the university, my interests had been wide-ranging. I found learning easy, but to commit myself to detail wasn't really my thing. I had always reached for the next interesting topic, always reacting positively to encouragement and recognition. I only understood much later that just grabbing opportunities has very little to do with self-determination.

But, if I wanted to make a career as a consultant, I would have to specialize. My boss gave me a choice: It was either "private banking" or "investment funds." But I wasn't really interested in either. It wasn't real enough for me. Too many figures, too much … hmm, tax-avoidance. But there wasn't really anything else for me in Luxembourg. What could I do? Move again? And where to? What on earth was I supposed to do—and where?

Many doors were open to me, but I didn't have a clue which one to choose. I was young and free but felt a complete lack of direction. Hadn't I reached my goal—a successful job abroad? Looking back, I know that Luxembourg was only a transit station on my hunt for recognition, on my endless search for more of it.

So far, my life had led me from one city to the next, one university to the next, one project to the next, one woman to the next—always without any commitment, always ready for the next kick. My job was really the equivalent of a lottery win for someone so new to the business, but it was killing me. I had felt burned out for a while.

But instead of taking things more slowly, I took on more and more major tasks. The next mega project for which they had already penciled me in was in connection with the German stock market. Together with a colleague, I frequently shuttled between Frankfurt and Luxembourg. We quickly grew fed up with anonymous hotels and planned to rent a lovely loft apartment for the coming months. It was a bargain compared with the hotel bills. We were about to pick up the keys when I hesitated. The Frankfurt project was going downhill. Again we fought our way from one deadline to the next. The stress never abated.

One night I was lying awake and asked myself what I was actually fighting for. Why perform all these complicated projections and process analyses? What is the purpose? I felt cut off from myself and somehow completely in the wrong place; there was a yearning in me for a task to which I could commit myself from the bottom of my heart. But what could that be? Maybe I needed some transcendent experience that would show me what was really important in life. I was desperately longing for a "compass." I'm not religious, but that night I sent a fervent prayer to heaven, asking fate for some advice. And fate answered very quickly and also pretty clearly ...

When I spoke to my parents on the phone the next day, telling them of my crisis, my dad said: "We're flying to Malaysia over Easter for a diving holiday. Why don't you come with us and relax a bit?" It sounded very tempting. During the previous year, I had seen my parents only sporadically, and some downtime would be very good for me. But how could I get two weeks off during these hectic times at work? My mother simply suggested: "Why don't you just ask them?" I did exactly that, and my boss agreed.

I was highly successful at work then, but at the same time without a proper direction. Something wasn't right in a life that on the surface looked so glamorous: a successful corporate consultant in an elegant suit rushing with a suitcase from one appointment to the next, lunching in top-rated restaurants. For years, my life had been restless, fleeting. The same applied to my relationships. I shuttled between noncommittal affairs and longer relationships without finding any fulfilment. Today I realize that I was in crisis already. At the time though, I only felt stuck.

Off to My Adventure

My parents and I flew to Sipadan in Malaysia, a dream of a tropical island a few kilometers off Borneo's northern Pacific coast. The sea around it is a paradise for divers. The coastal shelf falls steeply away for six hundred meters. The depths are patrolled by schools of barracuda you normally only meet far out in the ocean. Sipadan is particularly renowned as a breeding place for various kinds of turtles. They are protected, as they return to the beaches year after year to lay their eggs—one reason why the number of tourists on the island is strictly limited. I felt like Robinson Crusoe on his desert island. One could circle the island comfortably in half an hour, and we walked barefoot either on the fine sand or in the warm, lapping waves. On the inner part of the island, I came across an iguana, nearly a meter long. It was guarding its nest of eggs in a sandy hollow, and hissed a threat at me. Looking through my camera lens, I thought it would make an amazing shot.

But I enjoyed it even more when, one evening, the rangers from the turtle station called the tourists over to watch one of nature's miraculous sights: hundreds of baby turtles were hatching at the same time and raced across the beach to the safety of the ocean.

Several times a day we dived down to the immensely colorful landscape of the coral reef, just drifting in warm water, looking around in amazement. It was the perfect place for me. I managed to switch off at last, enjoying the simplicity of everything. Work and my worries vanished into the background, and the actual distance from my chaotic love life helped me relax.

On the evening that was to change my life—it was our tenth day on the island—my parents and I were lounging on deckchairs on the sundeck outside the open-air restaurant. It had been my idea, which later I would bitterly regret.

It was a moment of total relaxation and the highlight of a dream holiday. Holding an iced cocktail, I looked out to sea and listened to the lapping waves. A light breeze of salty sea air felt comfortably cool. My parents had put their feet up and smiled happily at each other. We talked about our afternoon activities and then clinked our glasses in praise of this perfect Easter Sunday.

If we had followed my parents' plan, we would have been ten meters away out in the water and ready for some night diving on the reef. But it would have been the fourth dive of the day, and it nearly felt like stress to me. So, in the afternoon, I had asked my parents to spend our Easter Sunday evening leisurely on land. They gave in and let the night diving session go.

Watching the sky at night was our TV. One minute the sky was a deep blood red; the next the stars were glittering so brightly that you felt a part of the cosmos. This abrupt change is typical for tropical countries. In front of us, some night divers let the air out of their jackets and sank down to another world. We watched as their lights slowly faded in the dark water. It was incredibly quiet, and my father murmured, "What a blessing to be allowed such a peaceful Sunday."

Then we heard panicky cries behind us, and the idyll collapsed. Everything happened very quickly.

When I turned around, I saw several armed men storming the restaurant. One of them had a rocket launcher on his shoulder. A second later, he loomed right behind me. Staring into the barrel of his bazooka, I tried to make sense of it all. Time seemed to stop. I felt my heart in my throat. Several gaunt and weedy looking men, partly masked, were waving semi-automatic weapons at us, calling "Police! Police!" But they didn't seem to be friendly and helpful at all, rather like fishermen and farmers from the fringes of the civilized world. We were chased toward the bungalows of the hotel complex. "Faster! Faster!" Their nervousness was palpable. They didn't seem sure of what they were doing, but that made them more dangerous. Armed weakness is much more dangerous than armed strength.

The men drove us, together with the other tourists and some hotel employees, past the bungalows toward the beach. I expected that they were about to rob us and ransack the bungalows.

In the pale moonlight, I made out two narrow wooden fishing boats. I felt the barrel of a gun in my back. My mother and I were pushed into one boat; my father into the other.

An American woman refused to get in. She couldn't swim and her fear of water was stronger than her fear of the men. Collapsing into the shallows she clung to her husband. Three men failed to get her into the boat. The situation threatened to escalate. The kidnappers were waving their weapons. Their body language said they were ready to kill. Suddenly, it seemed very possible that someone would be murdered in front of our eyes. But then the men let the couple go, pushed the boats deeper into the water, and started the outboard engines. The condition of the boats seemed to indicate a short journey. But that turned out to be wrong.

We huddled closely together, forty people in two boats, about the same number of victims and hijackers. I could hardly breathe from a combination of fear and being crammed in, at a loss as to what would happen next. Would they throw us into the water and shoot at us once we were further out? I was overcome by deep regret. Why hadn't we gone on the night dive?!

Somehow, I found some space between two fellow victims. My mother was crouching a few meters further down, leaning against the side of the boat. With a sobbing voice, she whispered, "I'm so sorry that you are here because of me. I shouldn't have persuaded you to come on this holiday."

Thoughts about guilt and fate. Should I have refused to be persuaded to come? What if we were on a different island today as my father had suggested? But suddenly, a completely different thought surfaced. Was this the hint from fate I had asked for? Then my wish had been granted!

The thought caused my body to tingle with a kind of euphoria. Maybe I was still slightly hazy from the cocktails, but all of a sudden, I saw the possibility of being on a journey toward myself. That I was going to learn something that would give me a compass for life.

The fear remained, but now I was also curious. Wide awake, I decided to memorize everything that happened from now on and to look for a deeper meaning. I gradually stopped bemoaning my fate and started to concentrate on how to best deal with the situation.

A Clear Purpose Gives You Strength

On that boat, I felt a clear purpose I had never experienced before, at least not in my job. I guessed that this journey would not only be very stressful but also life-threatening. But despite my fears, I knew exactly what I would be fighting for: my survival. Focusing on that goal, I gained inner clarity, and that gave me sufficient strength.

The hopelessness of the situation somehow had a liberating effect on me. There was only one direction. For the first time, I didn't have to make a difficult decision. When I recognized this clearly, it felt as if a burden was taken from me. All connections to my former life had been severed. Nobody could contact me here. The acute stress, my fundamental lack of direction at work, and the chaos of my relationships were far away. I felt strong and somehow in the right place—a feeling I had longed for since my childhood.

A Transcendent Experience

The kidnappers kept in touch between the two boats by light signals. My mother and I couldn't contact my father for hours, and were worried we would never see each other again. Everyone was deeply troubled, but on the outside, a certain calmness gradually set in. The sea was calm, there was a pleasant breeze, and the star-studded night sky was breathtaking. Life on board began to take some shape. I talked to the man next to me. We speculated about what would lie ahead of us. Our imaginations explored robbery, ritual executions, or being kidnapped for ransom. Fear was mirrored in every face.

The man sitting between me and my mother introduced himself as Seppo, saying he had only just arrived from Finland. He couldn't stop sobbing, buried his face in his hands, and kept repeating "No, no, no!" At some point, he put his head in my mother's lap. She comforted him by stroking his back and calmed herself down a bit as well.

It was oppressively tight on the boat. Most of the space was filled with petrol canisters, and it seemed that we were going on a long journey. We could hardly move. In the night we were drenched by spray; during the day we were exposed to the hot sun. We had nothing apart from the clothes we were wearing and had to relieve ourselves in the boat. Soon the stench became unbearable: a mixture of urine, saltwater, and petrol was lapping at our feet.

We didn't know then that we were heading toward an island called Jolo—part of the Sulu Archipelago in the southern part of the Philippines. Our kidnapping was the first crime of this type that crossed the border between Malaysia and the Philippines.

Soon I began my search for the meaning of it all. Hadn't I longed for something like this? A kick in the butt like back at school? But this was an adventure and a half! During the twenty hours at sea, I managed to accept my situation. Sipadan felt like a lifetime ago. I began to look ahead to this journey despite its very uncertain outcome.

In contrast with me, my mother had trouble dealing with the situation—particularly her own role in it. She kept blaming herself and whispered time and again, "I wish I hadn't said anything. You wouldn't have asked your boss for a holiday and wouldn't be here." I was deeply moved by the way my mother worried about her child's wellbeing, even in this perilous situation. This mother-son relationship was about to change dramatically throughout the upcoming events.

I reached out over Seppo's shoulder to touch my mother and comfort her. "Nothing happens without a reason. It will make sense at some point. Don't worry about me, I'm okay." But I realized that she kept imagining scenarios that would have kept us from ending up here. The spiral of thoughts was robbing her of all energy as she made a desperate attempt to turn back the clock and make everything disappear. But you cannot go back in time, so you should focus all your energy on how to make the best of the situation.

This is easier said than done. In such moments, it's invaluable to be able to put down your thoughts on paper, to free your head. It was one of the many crazy coincidences of our journey that we got hold of some paper and pencils. After about two weeks of captivity, I began to write down our experiences in a "hostage diary," and to process them at the same time. Scientists have established that some survivors of extreme situations develop a sense of gratitude for what happened to them and end up feeling enriched. I hadn't come that far, but I was determined to make the best of my situation.

"This is my attempt to write down and process the events of this ordeal in real time," I wrote in my "Jungle Diary." "I regret that I didn't have the means and the energy in the first few days to remember everything we went through step by step. Nevertheless, I want to write down as many details as possible and thus process them, because it's never too late."

Most of the hostages kept a diary. Seppo was an artist and expressed his experience in drawings. For me, writing the diary was a way to accept what was happening. After our release, it also helped me to recollect the events and to put them into perspective. It was a very valuable experience.

What Is Resilience?

Any crisis is demanding. It takes a lot out of us, especially while it's going on. But a crisis, in my view, also has a lot of positive aspects. We can learn from it and grow. It takes a lot of energy and inner strength for this to happen. This inner strength, called "resilience," is the personal spirit of resistance in individuals and systems, such as in teams and organizations, when they come under stress from outside and within. It also means the capacity to quickly and sustainably recover after an ordeal. To this day, however, there is no precise definition of what characteristics, capacities, or forms of behavior are included. The word resilience is derived from the Latin verb *resilire,* meaning to bounce back or rebound. It was first used in physics, during research on materials, and means the characteristic of a material to either keep its original shape under mechanical stress or to quickly revert to its original shape.

There are common examples in everyday life. Think of a spring. When we stretch it, that is, exert a power on it, it loses its shape. But its resilience is so great that it invariably returns to its original state as soon as the outside force is removed. It resists permanent deformation. In the end, it releases the power exerted on it and springs back to its original shape. Springs have very high resilience. Glass, on the other hand, has very low resilience. It breaks when force is exerted on it.

Since the 1950s, psychology has taken the term resilience on board. Of course, the original physical definition cannot be transferred to the human psyche. Our mind isn't made of material that can be deformed or bent out of shape mechanically. But the term makes sense in psychology to describe one's mental resistance under duress.

In the course of our lives, we meet with a variety of stresses of all intensities, but there is an equal number of individual strategies we use to overcome them. There is no general formula for how to deal with stress or grief, for example. What is helpful for one person may make things worse for another. Resilience always consists of a multitude of personal characteristics, learned skills, and situational behavior. The combination is just as individual as we all are.

That is the reason why it's so difficult to define resilience clearly. There are a number of definitions and models that often overlap. For the most part, they feature different factors, use different perspectives, or emphasize the importance of various characteristics and skills. They all struggle to clearly formulate a thorough understanding of this important psychological strength.

For example, Kalisch (2017) describes resilience as the "maintenance or rapid restoration of mental health during or after adversities." Masten (2016), however, emphasizes the aspect of adaptability. For her, resilience is "the capacity of a dynamic system to successfully adapt to interferences which threaten its function, viability, or development."

The psychotherapist Rosemarie Welter-Enderkin (2008) adds the perspective of developmental psychology, and understands resilience as "the capacity of men (...) to master crises within their lifetime with the help of personal and socially acquired resources and to use them as a starting point for development."

At their core, all the definitions have four critical phases for the management of stressors: dealing with stress, reducing stress, recovering after stress, and developing after stress. The first three factors help to master a crisis with strength, meaning to remain mentally healthy during an acute crisis. The fourth factor is helpful to get stronger through a crisis, to grow with it, and to be better equipped for future crises.

How that can happen successfully differs and depends on the model and perspective. A frequently used model is that of the "pillars," combining helpful characteristics and skills. I call them "protective factors" because they protected me in the jungle and time and again in my personal and working life. My own most important protective factors are acceptance, optimism, stress management, self-efficacy, social support, and fitness and discipline. Every person has his or her own mixture of these or other elements. In dealing with stress, it's interesting that a distinct strength in one competence can balance out a weakness in another. It's therefore not necessary to be in total control of every single protective factor. Rather, whatever protective factors are already present, derived from personal resources and strategies, can be applied in a focused and sustainable way.

It's well worth exploring one's own resilience. There are multiple studies offering evidence that resilience not only enables one to deal with stress successfully, but that it can also have additional positive effects. People with a high level of resilience have significantly fewer physical ailments, recover faster after a stressful episode, and adapt to changes more quickly. They suffer less from anxiety and depression and boast a higher level of overall satisfaction with life. Resilience clearly has a positive effect on the physical, mental, and social wellbeing of people.

What's best is that you can *learn* to be resilient and then develop this attribute! The protective factors listed above can be a solid framework for this. It's not only about finding out about this or that competence, but rather recognizing one's own potential, resources, and strategies when dealing with stress, so as to use them and develop them further.

It makes sense that an early approach to resilience can be valuable, and it is a high priority to encourage it in child and adolescent psychology. Also, people in mentally stressful occupations, so-called risk groups—such as the emergency and rescue services or intensive care hospital workers—can benefit from a targeted promotion of resilience.

During the past few years, I have sadly learned that big companies largely believe resilience to be the employee's responsibility and expect their workers to endure growing pressure and stress. Often, the priority is not in keeping and restoring the employee's health, but rather in promoting their performance and efficiency (in the company's interest) under adverse conditions. To my mind, this is shortsighted and potentially counterproductive. Suffering from stress is a serious warning signal for possible crises. It's like a smoke alarm. As soon as it starts beeping, we shouldn't simply take out the battery to stop it, we should look for the cause. Smoke = approaching crisis or stress; fire = acute crisis; or false alarm = individual resilience? Only then do we tend to ask whether it's necessary to strengthen the individual resistance of the employee.

Or is it perhaps better to change some of the conditions that caused the stress? To make employees more durable is almost never the right response and can be counterproductive. What would happen if the smoke alarm didn't respond to an actual fire? There might be considerable damage as a consequence. For that reason, management is often asked to deal sustainably with their employees and not burn them out; to take signals of stress seriously in order to remove the conditions for it early.

I am convinced that there's not just one correct way of dealing with stress, and at the end of each chapter will give you an inspiration regarding how to integrate my insights and experiences into your own life at home and at work. Please explore what is relevant for you, and notice whether your experience is completely different than mine.

Inspiration for the Protective Factor "Acceptance"

In order to deal with a crisis, you first must accept it as such. It's absolutely human to respond to a difficult situation by asking "Why me?" especially when dealt a severe blow. But what has happened cannot be undone. It's helpful to accept the new situation as quickly as possible and to make the best of it. Writing a diary, for example, supports this process. When you document the events, your own position in it becomes more real and helps to make you capable of dealing with it. You also clear your head for the challenges ahead. It's been scientifically proven that acceptance is an important protective factor of resilience. At the end of the book, you'll find more suggestions about how to strengthen your capacity for acceptance, as well as other protective factors.

Everything Will Be Okay

Acceptance helps you to take the past on board and face present challenges. A second important protective factor is optimism. Optimism gives us strength and helps us, particularly in difficult times, not to lose the belief in a positive future. If you have both these factors, you will be well equipped in a crisis—they are both forward-looking.

Of course, it sounds really simple. You just have to accept the situation and look ahead with confidence. But try to give that advice to someone who is in the middle of an existential crisis, and you might get a slap in the face. Each crisis is different, as is each human being. And each of us has a different way of dealing with things. But people can learn from and inspire each other.

In my life, time and again I've had the good fortune to meet inspiring people. A long time after the kidnapping, I worked as a manager for technical orthopedic centers. I met many people who had recently had an arm or leg amputated. They were all in a deep crisis. Life forced them to adapt to a new reality and a changed body. Many couldn't or wouldn't accept their fate. But as long as they wished for their intact body back, their whole energy was rooted in the past. Only when they were ready to make the most of their new situation did they invest all their strength into the challenging process of rehabilitation. Personal visualizations played a vital part in this process. It was important for these people to take their eyes off the past and look ahead to the future.

A particularly inspiring example of the power of positive thinking came from a Middle Eastern professor who had lost both her legs in a car bomb attack. Technically, her treatment was complicated, but she was optimistic and fought like a lioness. She was eventually successful because she never lost sight of her vision of the future. "I will return to university as a professor—standing up. I want to be a role model and to encourage my students during these difficult times and to demonstrate that the terrorists won't win." Months later, when I came across a photo of this woman actually standing in front of her class, I had goosebumps all over.

In contrast to the professor, we hostages on Jolo could still hope to come out of our ordeal alive. Apart from acceptance, optimism greatly helped us to get through it. But we could never take it for granted, because the circumstances gave very little reason to be optimistic.

In the Midst of Jungle Warfare

After the long and arduous boat journey, we finally got to land. Exhausted, we trudged through a mangrove swamp.

Time and again, our naked feet landed on pointed stones in the knee-deep mud. Seppo sustained a painful injury on one foot. Once on dry land again, we tried to stop the bleeding with algae, but we had to go on to the "headquarters," as a short, middle-aged man who introduced himself as "Commander Robot" told us. He seemed to be in charge, and was one of the few armed men able to speak a bit of English.

There was a hint of hope that once we arrived at wherever we were going, we would be able to take a shower and get something to eat and drink. After about ten hours trekking through the dense vegetation, we arrived at our destination in darkness, completely exhausted. It was a hideaway in the middle of the jungle. No trace of a headquarters as I had imagined it. We were led to a primitive bamboo hut on stilts without electricity or water, with just one candle and a rough ladder to climb up.

I was horrified and felt very down. It was stiflingly hot, and the air was thick with the smoke from a firepit. Swarms of mosquitoes buzzed in and landed on my sweaty skin. I asked Commander Robot: "Toilet?" At first, he looked at me with irritation, then amusement, and gestured to the surrounding area by spreading out his arms. Accompanied by some armed men with flashlights, I went into the darkness to relieve myself. On the way, we passed a few small groups of young men, squatting on the ground in the light of improvised oil lamps that looked like Molotov cocktails. Hammocks were strung between the trees, some with a colorful plastic sheet above. These were the quarters of many armed men who apparently had expected our arrival.

They gathered around us, staring curiously, holding rifles, munition belts slung over their shoulders. They talked in an aggressive-sounding language, and some laughed out loud. We felt like helpless prey in a lion's den. And that's exactly what we were. Eventually we learned that we had been kidnapped by Islamist rebels and taken to the Philippine island of Jolo, northeast of Sipadan.

The rebels belonged to the terrorist organization Abu Sayyaf (which roughly translates as "sword fighters"), also known as Harakat al-Islamiyya. The group was founded in 1991 by the Afghan fighter Abdurajak Abubakar Janjalani, and named after its founder. For us, the rebel group Abu Sayyaf appeared like a grotesque bunch of religious fanatics, political extremists, and greedy bandits.

The Abu Sayyaf group originated in the Moro National Liberation Front (MNLF), but had found the political aims of the MNLF too moderate, as it had signed a peace agreement with the Philippine central government that gave the Moros a certain autonomy over areas on Mindanao and in the South Philippine archipelago. The political aim of Abu Sayyaf was complete independence from the federation of the Philippines and the creation of an Islamic caliphate. Janjalani had been shot by police in the Philippines two years before our abduction. This might have been an additional motive for the approximately two hundred core members of Abu Sayyaf to plan a particularly spectacular operation.

The leader of our group, Galib Andang, was called Commander Robot because, during the skirmishes with the army, he had kept on fighting like a robot even when he was hit by bullets. He would have been a policeman, if he hadn't been so short. This grievance is said to have driven him to take up arms with the rebels. Together with the inscrutable Mujib Susukan, he held a position of authority over several hundred rebels, which were recruited from the villages on the island as and when needed. Apart from a few fighters trained in terrorist camps, they were farmers' sons who had very little contact with civilization but possessed a great enthusiasm for weapons.

There were also some child soldiers among the five hundred fighters surrounding us. Their innocent faces were in stark contrast to the weapons they were carrying: modern American M16 assault rifles. We managed a conversation with one of the boys. He told us that they had given him an amulet that he was always supposed to wear. The recruiter had told him that it had great power and would deflect all enemy bullets. Child soldiers also accompanied us to the river. They were to ensure that we wouldn't be "conquered" by another rebel group or a rival clan, because, after all, they wanted to get a ransom for us one day. Abu Sayyaf was a guerrilla troop perfectly adapted to jungle warfare. A large part of the population in the region regarded them as soldiers for liberation, fighting against the oppression of the Christian-dominated government and its military.

In my view, religious aims and convictions played only a minor role with our kidnappers. I never felt as though I was the hostage of a religious group. For me, they were all terrorists and bandits who abused innocent people. As human shields, we were guaranteeing their safety against military action by the Philippine army. We feared for our lives on the front line as several fights between the warring factions broke out. But something made us even more frightened than the heavy artillery: it was the machetes that everyone around us carried. In peacetime, the Jolo farmers use them for weeding or cutting bamboo. But the rebels also sometimes used them on their hostages when their demands for ransom weren't met. This thought alone made our blood freeze.

The Sword of Damocles Above Our Heads

In a single night, without any anticipation and completely involuntarily, we found ourselves in a changed reality that couldn't have been stranger and more hostile. We were in the middle of a guerrilla war and in the middle of a jungle. More or less unprotected, we were exposed to poisonous insects and the tropical climate. Malnourishment and a lack of personal hygiene led to illnesses, such as infected wounds, which stayed untreated because of a lack of medical support. But the greatest threat to our lives was not the unpredictability of nature or the military conflict, but the volatility of our tormentors.

In our first camp, we met Patrick, a Philippine hostage who had been abducted a few weeks earlier on Jolo but was released a few days after our arrival. He told us that the Abu Sayyaf group decapitated their hostages if their demands weren't met. At first, we refused to believe it. But then Patrick showed us an article in a Philippine daily he had been secretly given by someone in the nearby village. It was a report about decapitations and shootings of women, children, and priests by the Abu Sayyaf on the neighboring island of Basilan.

We were now haunted by horror pictures. In addition to the physical threats, there was now a psychological one that was no less dangerous. Catastrophizing, a whirlpool of negative thinking, is the natural enemy of optimism. When your thoughts revolve around a horror scenario, you lose the most important thing of it all: hope. And exactly that happened to my mother. She had a dream of how I, her son, was decapitated in front of her. To spare me the anguish, she only told me about it after our release.

This dream occurred again and again to my mother, and it pulled the rug from under her feet, at first mentally, then physically as well. She didn't only suffer from panic attacks and anxiety, but also from extreme back pain and high blood pressure. She had to learn about the power of mental images in a very painful way. Luckily, there were also examples among us about the influence of positive visualizations on one's attitude.

The Positive Power of Imagination

Top athletes swear by the power of their visions. Even before their start, they play a kind of film inside their heads of how they hit the finish line first or beat their own record in the high jump. Motivational trainers often repeat the importance of clear visions of success, expressed in sayings such as "The key to success is to focus on things we want—not on the things we fear" (Brian Tracy). If you can envision your goal, your aspiration, with all your senses, then your determination to find a way to victory increases. On Jolo, I learned that positive images not only help to realize dreams. They also give you the strength to get through a nightmare.

The fear of dying was with us during the whole time of our captivity. But apart from a few occasions, I never lost the confidence that all would be good in the end. "Everything will be okay," was my mantra. It worked particularly powerfully when I envisaged the time after our release. The pleasant thoughts and calm images comforted me and gave me hope for freedom and a return to normality. I imagined how I would go to a café in Luxembourg, order a cappuccino, read the paper, and listen to the music in the background. And then I would be met by a good friend and tell him all about the crazy times on Jolo.

This scenario for me is the epitome of freedom—simply to do what I want, without any thrills. Another longing focused on seeing my brother Dirk, hugging him, and then going for a beer with him. Both images gave me strength and enabled me to remain positive, and they became a reality after my release.

The other hostages also imagined what they would do once they were back in freedom. When facing death, most people have a "bucket list," and we all wrote a list of things in our diaries we were determined to do before our life was over. Jolo was a kind of YOLO experience for us—an acronym for "You Only Live Once." Jolo starkly reminded us of the transience of life and our dreams. My father had loved his job as a geography teacher from the bottom of his heart, but his secret dream had always been to be a travel writer. On Jolo, he started planning to later publish his diary to let people know about his experiences.

Callie and Monique from South Africa decided to have children once they were free again. They also made drawings for the landscaping of their garden at home. The future visions of the other hostages ranged from traveling, to changing their job, to visiting fine restaurants. The visualizations of how our life was to continue gave us all much strength. Other items on my list were "to be a pianist tinkling in a bar" and "to really fall in love and have a family."

Faith Helps

Apart from the worldly visions, faith played an important role in difficult moments. When you see your fate as a result of God's will or as part of a general plan, it's easier to accept the present. In a crisis, to have faith in a god gives people the confidence that in the end everything will be alright. Many hostages gained strength from their faith.

My father had always been a devout Christian. In the first hours of our kidnapping when we were sailing toward an unknown destiny, he saw three shooting stars in the night sky. For him it was a sign from God that all would be good. He was utterly convinced that the three of us would survive. I'm not particularly familiar with the Bible and also not a church goer, but my education was Christian, and I consider myself a spiritual person. I believe in the power of praying. "Prayer" is what I had called my wish for fate to intervene, which I thought might have found resonance somewhere in the universe and propelled me into this dubious adventure. The belief alone that I might have influenced my fate, turned me from a victim to a person who shapes his destiny. This belief, too, helped me to accept what was happening.

I'm also convinced that praying for other people can be effective. When my parents and I heard that in Germany many people in churches and prayer groups were praying for our release, we weren't only grateful but also firmly believed in the power of this spiritual support.

And another thing: In many printed emails that we got ahold of in various ways in our hostage camp, strangers wished us the strength to overcome the ordeal. "Keep going!" we read time and again. We felt practically obliged to survive the hostage situation. In several conversations with my parents, we agreed that we couldn't possibly disappoint the many well-wishers. We simply had to remain positive for their sake and stick out the captivity until it was over.

Led by the practicing Christian, Callie, several prayer groups formed in our hostage camp. Every night, he invited us to take part in the "sunset prayer." We followed him, depending on our own mood. As we spent most of the time with our kidnappers in hideaways in the woods, their constant presence and their blaring transistor radios soon turned into a mental torture. With time and with growing trust, the rebels allowed us to move away from the camp for a short distance. So, we went to a quiet place for praying, to a clearing or around a fire. I had expected the prayers to be fervent, such as: "Dear God, please get us out of here quickly!" But Callie found words of gratefulness, such as: "Thank you, dear Lord, that we're still alive," or "thank you for the food that we received today!" Then he invited everyone to say a thank-you prayer as well. It was amazing how many things we could feel gratitude for in that miserable situation: "Thank you that so many people pray for us"; "thank you that there are negotiations for our release;" "thank you that there was no military attack today." This routine made us aware of all the positive aspects that due to the stress and fear would otherwise have been overlooked. At the end, we held hands and went back to our day-to-day hostage life, but filled with hope. Apart from the mental benefit, this ritual also had a good influence on team building.

Some of the Muslim hostages joined their captors in their prayers, all facing Mecca. There were only a few Muslims among them, but we would very often be awakened at sunrise by the call of "Allahu Akbar."

Inspiration for the Protective Factor "Optimism"

In difficult times, optimistic people trust that the situation will improve. They focus on the good sides and things that work. They assume a positive result of their own actions and thus show a higher readiness for activeness and endurance. In their responses, they experience more positive emotions than pessimistic people. This again not only has a positive effect on their mental wellbeing, but also on their health. In research on the psychology of health, a positive correlation between optimism and mental and physical health is seen as a given (see: J. Bengel and L. Lyssenko [2012]).

In many ways, optimism is an enormous source of strength:

- Mentally, optimism helps to overcome misfortunes more easily and more quickly. In studies with victims of earthquakes, the affected people with a high score on the optimism scale showed significantly fewer signs of stress. Further research evidenced that optimists recovered faster from serious injuries and intensive care, and after their recuperation showed fewer symptoms of anxiety and depression.
- Physically, a positive attitude to life strengthens the general health. A study by a German health insurer showed that optimistic students under exam pressure were less susceptible to infections than less positive students.
- Optimists have, thanks to their positive attitude about life, a larger social network. This again helps them to deal with difficult times.

The good news is that optimism can be learned. One step toward it is the *ritual of gratitude*. In the evening, before you drop off, remember three things during the day for which you can be grateful. It's best to say them aloud or write them down. Regardless of how stressful your situation might have been, there will always be three things for which you can be grateful. Doing this, you focus your attention on things that have pleased you and trigger positive emotions, which in turn increase your sense of well-being.

The ritual makes sense especially when you're already in a relaxed state. A ritual deepens when practiced regularly and will become a ready source of strength in difficult times. In other words, the fire brigade doesn't start practicing when the fire has started.

Keep Your Head

It's well known and scientifically proven that an optimistic attitude helps in dealing with a crisis. There are quite a few proverbs and sayings about the power of positive thinking that express this wisdom: "The glass is half full not half empty"; "A cheerful mind does half the work"; and "Faith can move mountains"; to name a few. Those sayings give us courage in difficult times. So far, so good. But sometimes optimism dulls our view of the real dangers. And that can be extremely dangerous.

For me, positive thinking once nearly led to my financial ruin. After a long downtime, my bank balance was dangerously low. I urgently needed another job. Of course, I assumed that, with my amazing résumé, it wouldn't be a problem. For the labor market in those days, it was kind of normal to send out about a hundred applications. I had sent out two and was promptly invited to interview for both positions.

I was so sure of myself! In my head, both jobs were mine already, and I didn't spend any more efforts on further applications. I duly got the invitations for the second round of interviews. Yes, it was a done deal! My friends advised me to send out further applications, just in case.

But I remained optimistic: "You wait and see; I'll be offered at least one of the positions."

Six weeks later, I was taught a harsh lesson. I was rejected for both jobs. That meant I was back at square one and had lost precious time when I should have written more job applications. What followed was a difficult phase with several failed applications and mounting debts. And the moral of this is, if the danger hasn't passed, you better take it seriously. Soccer players would say, "A match has ninety minutes." And what is correct in the workplace and in soccer was even more valid in the jungle. Because it was about our very lives.

Life-Threatening Times

The uncertainty was one of the hardest things on Jolo. We had no idea whether we would leave the island alive or not, and if alive, when would that be? At any moment, we could be either shot or released. The more desperate and threatening a situation is, the more fear and uncertainty you feel. The greater the desperation, the more tempted you are to cling to illusions—like someone dying of thirst in the desert who chases a mirage and euphorically calls "Water, water!" before collapsing in the sand. Our mirage was freedom.

The optimists among us expected to be released soon. "It won't last more than a week," they said. But the week went by, and we were still captive. The disappointment was huge; the mood rock bottom.

Time and again, we allowed ourselves to believe the hostage takers and their alleged plans. Time and again, we asked, "When will we be released?" And the answer was always, "Soon, very soon. Maybe tomorrow. If not tomorrow, then the day after tomorrow."

In the beginning, we all believed it—and became hopeful! But hope in a difficult situation is far too precious to waste on cheap comforts or to sacrifice to obvious self-deceit. But that's what the optimists did. It's better to call them "euphorics." Even weeks after the forced journey across the sea, they still fell for the kidnapper's ruses. At every rumor of an imminent release, they became euphoric. "Only two more days, then we'll be free." Two days later, they fell into a big black hole of low mood because again it hadn't happened. It was a dangerous up and down of emotions and went on for weeks, and then, for months.

This life-threatening, nail-biting experience was devastating for all the hostages, but it was worst for the optimists, because time and again, their mood changed from euphoria to depression. Some developed serious suicidal ideations. They got lost in their feelings instead of keeping their head.

In a crisis and in difficult times, it's a veritable art to keep one's head. It means that you fall prey neither to fear nor to euphoria, but you stay realistic and optimistic at the same time, believing in a good outcome while remaining equally prepared for a long and hard struggle.

This attitude helps not only in coping with a crisis, but also in gaining a victory, even against a feared opponent. Soccer trainers drum it into the players never to be fearful of the next opponent, but respectful. "This path will not be an easy one, it will be rocky and hard," are the lyrics by Xavier Naidoo, whose song became the unofficial anthem of the German soccer team during the 2006 World Cup. In this sense, the national team prepared emotionally for each game, with the result that this World Cup turned out to be a *Sommermärchen* (summer fairy tale)—maybe an equivalent to Liverpool winning the Champions League or the Dallas Cowboys winning the Super Bowl.

Positive Thinking Can Be Deadly

Frustrated expectations can present a big risk to positive thinking. Some of the hostages were driven by them to the brink of their endurance and nearly to suicide. It's even more dangerous when people with unbridled optimism block out the real risks instead of preparing for them. For us, it was vitally necessary for our survival not only to prepare mentally but also practically for a long and dangerous time in the jungle. We had to ration food, seek supplies, keep fit. At the core of it, discipline was needed, and the mantra was "Don't give up!"

In some respects, we assessed our situation very differently. Again and again, we had difficult discussions about decisions regarding more than just one person. For example, I initially shared precious empty rice bags with my parents. We had restyled them as a means for transporting things, but also as sleeping mats. The dilemma arose after a long hike to a new camp. Shall we cut up the rice bag to have a bigger mat for sleeping, or shall we keep it intact to use as a bag again during a possible further hike? My father was absolutely sure. "This is our last camp. From here we will be released." But I thought, "Who's to know?"

Among the hostages, I was considered to be a more skeptical person and sometimes even a pessimist—whereas, I always thought of myself as an optimist. My diary entry of May 23, 2000 describes this. "We never know anything and have to remain optimistic, but at the same time expect everything. Whether or when we will be released is completely uncertain. At this point, two days or two months are an equally realistic estimate."

People who expect the worst are often regarded as pessimists. But they simply deal with facts and risks in a realistic way and take precautions accordingly, so in case of a deteriorating situation, they can be as positive as the optimists. I compare this with a fire drill, which is not meant to frighten people either—quite the opposite. A fire drill can reassure you, because it's for your own safety and might save other lives. We too had to be prepared; otherwise, things could easily be life-threatening.

At the beginning of our captivity, we all were fairly optimistic, but not able to calculate the risks realistically. We knew that the Philippine military was positioned in a wide circle around us, but couldn't imagine they would attack. On the tenth day, however, the soldiers around our camp started firing from close range.

In a panic, we fled into the jungle leaving all our belongings behind. For two days and a night, we ran through the jungle, mostly barefooted and crazy with dehydration. To march in flip-flops in the moonlight over slippery paths through the underbrush is risky enough, but without flip-flops, it was a disaster. With every blind step, we feared to step on pointed stones, thorny sticks, or poisonous insects. It was extremely dangerous, because we didn't have any medical equipment.

Thirst was the second risk, but that was our own fault because we had left the water bottles behind when we fled. The stifling heat—in the nighttime too—felt like an extended time in the sauna. After several kilometers, we all hit our inner brick wall. My mother fared even worse, and collapsed. She was so dehydrated that she simply keeled over.

Due to many lucky coincidences, no one died, although some of us were injured. My mother was transported on a donkey we took over from a villager. Some of our belongings were brought over by the rebels. And in a moment of total exhaustion and completely out of the blue, we received the first aid package of battle rations from the French army—how fitting in a guerrilla war.

We had survived with only a few bruises. The optimists said, "Phew, we made it," and dropped to the ground exhausted. The realists said, "It can happen again," and organized their belongings in order not to lose them again next time.

Stress — a Helper for Survival

In a crisis, there are two very dangerous states of mind: catastrophizing and euphoria. In both cases, the performance suffers. In the first case, it is because of too much stress; in the second case, because of too little stress. Tension stimulates people to a certain point. Afterwards, the performance drops again. According to the Yerkes-Dodson law, there is a u-shaped curve of efficiency in relation to tension. My mother was a clear case for catastrophizing. The recurring horror images of decapitations triggered panic and anxiety in her and made her collapse physically and mentally. She had too much stress, while the so-called (by me) naïve optimists sometimes did not have enough of it. They turned euphoric upon hearing rumors of an imminent release and became too relaxed in dangerous situations. Both states are equally problematic; you either get lost in your feelings or, as I call it, lose your head. Because, in a crisis, it's important to manage your own stress level to see that there's not too much stress, but not too little either.

Stress has a bad reputation. But it's a physical response that enabled our ancestors to survive. In this context, you often hear the example of facing a saber-toothed tiger in the wild. If our ancestors hadn't experienced stress, we wouldn't be here. Without stress, they would have come to the easy and optimistic assessment: "It won't do anything; it only wants to play ..."

But what if the tiger is hungry? In that case, a sophisticated mechanism comes into play, when the body releases adrenalin, which in turn raises blood sugar, and increases blood pressure and muscle tone. The body system is put into a state of alarm and made ready for the two options—the only ones appropriate when facing a sabre tooth tiger: fight or flight.

So far, the theory. But how did we, the hostages, deal with our stress? There were no sudden appearances of sabre-toothed tigers in our jungle, but rather, hundreds of fighters armed to their teeth. In this situation, neither fighting nor fleeing were realistic options. To fight our kidnappers would have been suicidal. And to sneak away, out of the jungle, with twenty-one other hostages wasn't realistic either. We had no way of knowing where we were, and the island appeared to be teeming with rebels and sympathizers. The jungle itself was the perfect prison warden. That's why we fought or fled in our own specific way, in the figurative sense.

Imaginary Escapes

Physically we were captives, but in our heads, we were free—at least at times. We all had our own way of taking some downtime from the demanding reality of being a hostage. We dreamed of a different world, especially when the stress was building up. Sometimes this could be quite grotesque, and quite often I remembered the touching, tragical comedy "Life is Beautiful" by Roberto Benigni. Benigni plays a Jewish inmate of a concentration camp who tries to shield his son from the cruel reality by suggesting to him in a humorous way that the whole scenario was a complex game. They would have to strictly abide by the rules to win it and get the prize of a real tank.

When the stress built up, we became quite inventive. Sometimes it helped to whistle in the dark. On one of our many treks by day or night, Marie, a French hostage, once started whistling with exhaustion and fear. This appeared surreal to us, as we had to expect an attack by the Philippine army any time. But in moments like that, whistling can actually help to release the tension—as kettles do …

Others focused on the nature around us, which indeed was very beautiful. Stéphane from France specialized in insects and discovered some giant ants in a dead tree trunk. Above our heads, there was also a lot to see: monkeys, flying foxes, and parrots. It was an ideal place for birdwatching—that's how Callie from South Africa saw it. He went out on research excursions whenever he could.

We also went traveling in our minds. Quite often we also dreamed of lovely food. We described our favorite dishes in all their delicious details until we salivated. But those lovely moments vanished quickly when reality set in and we got our usual portion of rice. From time to time, however, we received aid packages with delicious food. After two weeks of eating rice boiled in river water, I treated myself to a piece of fudge on a night trek. It seemed to cause an explosion of my taste buds, and for a moment, I was catapulted back home. It was wonderful!

The Asian hostages gained a lot of strength from meditation. The person meditating is not meant to zone out and forget reality, but rather meditates to disrupt the stream of negative thoughts. I had already spotted Abi, a hostage from the Philippines who had been on the boat. During the whole journey of twenty hours, he simply sat there without moving a muscle. Several times I wondered whether he was still alive. I also considered whether he was part of the kidnapping gang because he appeared so unaffected.

Reading material was a very welcome distraction in our camp. We received books, newspapers, and magazines by mail. It's hard to believe, but at some point, we actually received parcels in the middle of the jungle. The rebels and their sympathizers brought the packets from the island's capital—but it wasn't a reliable service. The favorite reading was women's magazines, even for the men. Compared to our situation, they were so wonderfully trivial. Aida, the Filipina, devoured one issue of *Reader's Digest* after the other.

Sedatives were another popular means of reducing stress. I preferred cigarettes, which I could organize via my bodyguard. I started smoking after about a month of captivity. That was my escape from the demanding life as a hostage and gave me a little hit in our situation, which again and again appeared hopeless. Funnily enough, the brand name of the cigarettes I got hold of was called "Hope."

Near one of our camps, was a little dammed-up river. In this pool, my mother floated on her back, her ears under water. Those were the only moments she felt peaceful, without continuously hearing or fearing shootings. But after she came up again, the first shots she heard shocked her even more.

Some of us tried to sleep as much as possible. We escaped into slumber, put in earplugs and a cloth over our eyes, and dreamed the time away. But it was like in other difficult situations in life, when you wake up, everything is just as miserable as before, and you sink into an even deeper black hole.

One of the most effective ways of escaping was gallows humor. The more hopeless the situation was, the more we protected ourselves by being ironic.

The Last Exit: Gallows Humor

Sometimes people are quite irritated when I tell them that gallows humor had helped me during the kidnapping. Humor? In your situation? They assume that it can't have been very dangerous at all … but it was exactly the opposite. Just like the flippant comments by some people on the way to their execution, I only really understood the value of gallows humor when I felt close to death myself.

The negotiations about our release had stalled. The kidnappers constantly made new and more challenging demands. The negotiators on the opposite side held on to their option of a military solution. When the talks escalated, the negotiators broke off the process for a while, calling it a "cooling-off" phase.

A short time afterwards, representatives of the radical arm of the Aby Sayyaf group from the island of Basilan came to visit. Their leader, Abu Sabaya, positioned himself coolly in front of our bamboo hut and explained the situation, not mincing his words. "If no ransom is paid or the military attacks one more time, we will decapitate you."

At that moment I heard myself whisper involuntarily, "Marc, don't lose your head now!" It was as if someone held a gun to my head, but I would just arrange my tie nicely before I would be shot. Somehow completely crazy, but very effective. Gallows humor doesn't resolve problems, but at least it decreases the tension.

Just as crazy was the situation when, for the second time, we were attacked by the Philippine army. In no way was it meant to be an attempt to liberate us. To put pressure on the kidnappers, the army fired from all directions toward us for what felt like an eternity. Rifle salvos hissed through the air, banana leaves and tree bark were riddled with holes. Some grenades whizzed around us, announcing themselves by their typical whining noise. The kidnappers tried to get us out of the firing line and ordered me and some other hostages to jump into a large hollow in the ground. At least we were protected now from the rifle shots and splinters. The artillery shooting continued like a kind of Russian Roulette. We feared for our lives. I looked at the five rebels who had taken position around our hollow, either to protect us or to keep us from escaping. They seemed to be experienced fighters with a special task: keeping the hostages safe. Their experience was easily detectable. One had only one arm, another an eye patch. Another one had half his jaw missing, presumably blown away in a gunfight. Now, I'm definitely not a person who makes fun of other people's looks or disabilities, but at that moment, I involuntarily found the situation so comical that I shouted down into our hole, "That's not an elite troupe, it's a freakshow!"

Stéphane couldn't stop giggling, and we all laughed compulsively and unstoppably, like in a fit. My mother didn't laugh, though; she was frightened by my behavior and thought I might lose my head. She wasn't completely wrong. But maybe the laughter saved me from going totally crazy.

Because of this experience, today I can better understand why some professionals, such as paramedics and surgeons, often come up with very cynical comments. They're not making fun of others, but have to deal with the stress of their surroundings. It actually is quite a good self-protection.

Gallows humor doesn't only help in life-threatening situations, but also in the day-to-day normal craziness. Wikipedia's description is very apt: "A situation that makes light of a subject matter that is generally considered taboo, particularly subjects that are normally considered serious or painful to discuss." In that sense, humor helped us time and again to reduce the terror of our dangerous situation and make it more bearable.

The local radio station played the same song lyrics time and again. We felt if we had to listen one more time to "Please release me, let me go" or "We had joy, we had fun, we had seasons in the sun," it would drive us crazy. In the end, we decided to make noise too and started singing songs in the middle of the night. My father came up with new lyrics to the Beatles song *Yellow Submarine,* and so we all sang "We all live in the jungle of JOLO …" In the beginning, our kidnappers found it funny, but that soon stopped. But we were having fun or at least enjoyed the feeling that we could get to them somehow …

One graphic example of gallows humor involved our

food. When again we had a meager meal of rice, we had to actually force ourselves to eat, and encouraged each other with jokes like "Come on, let's feed the worms, they must be hungry." We all had worms after a while because of the lack of hygiene.

Fighting Within Our Limits

Escaping into your mind only protects you temporarily from going crazy when you are in danger of losing it. Returning to our oppressing and life-threatening reality often meant coming back to earth with a hard bump.

Other than escapism, the stress reaction of fighting can actually help to make a difficult situation better. But even if each of us had possessed a machine gun and munition, we wouldn't have stood a chance against the hundreds of trained guerrilla fighters. The rebels knew that too and often left their weapons lying around. We had no way of escaping, and definitely not by violent means. But we tried by peaceful means to influence them to set us free soon. A few times, international journalists were invited to the camp because the rebels were actively trying to get media attention. We made use of this opportunity by appealing fervently to the government to stop the military assaults and to take up negotiations again.

We didn't only fight for our release, but also for better conditions in our captivity. Our natural enemy was the rainforest, and we were without protection from the frequent rain. Most of the time, we lived on bamboo platforms. They were built on stilts to protect us from poisonous insects, but didn't have a roof for shelter. Once we were drenched through by a tropical rainstorm that lasted all night. Our engineers, Risto and Stéphane, built a kind of roof out of bamboo and plastic sheets, which clearly enhanced our life. A gutter made from a split and scraped-out bamboo cane had a brilliant effect. With it, we caught rainwater in an empty petrol canister and had a water supply for drier times.

Inspiration for the Protective Factor "Stress Management"

There's one motto in a crisis: "Keep your head!" When you begin to be euphoric in uncertain times, you should ask yourself, is the danger really over? Have I bagged that job because I've been invited for an interview? Or shall I apply for other positions to be on the safe side? This also helps with too much stress. Breathe consciously, observe your feelings and thoughts, but don't follow them or let them go. And if all that doesn't work, there's always gallows humor.

Helping Helps in a Crisis

Sooner or later, we all experience a crisis. People lose their job or a loved one. Others suffer a serious illness or have an accident. Often, they feel like victims and ask "Why me?" This is a very natural response, but it makes dealing with the crisis much more difficult. If you feel powerless and feel like surrendering, your fear propels you into a negative spiral. Among other things, the art of keeping one's head means to be aware of your options in order to handle the crisis. By doing something, a positive and strengthening feeling sets in that things are at least partly in your control. You utilize your own resources to find a solution that might improve the situation. Those resources can be former experiences you now remember, special competencies or practical skills. Everyone is good at something, and everyone has experienced success at some point. Once you take the initiative, you trigger a positive cycle.

There are, of course, knocks and hopeless situations that one's actions can't really influence or undo. But there's always *something* that you can do. And that makes you feel good! For example:

- I lost my job — I write applications for a new one.
- I lost my partner — I comfort my children.
- My house burned down — I call the insurance company.
- I have a serious illness — I share my experience with others.

Sometimes even little things can help:

- The bank balance is low, I have lost customers — I prepare to acquire new ones, tidy up my desk, and sharpen the pencils.

Everyone has his or her own way of dealing with difficult situations. Everyone is able to do something they are good at. The main thing is, do it! Being active gives strength and reduces fear.

That certainly applied to us on Jolo.

Being Active Builds Strength

Our fate was in the hands of our kidnappers. They were masters over our life and death, over our freedom and captivity. We couldn't escape from this situation but were able to transform it and improve it in our own way. By fighting for better conditions, we reduced some sources of stress. For example, we improved our lot when we built a roof against the constant rain, a gutter for drinking water, and so on. The actual advantages were enormous. We had taken our fate into our own hands. We were useful and felt competent, each to their own abilities and in their own way. Our engineers, Stéphane and Risto, constructed lots of useful things out of bamboo. Marie, the paramedic, dealt with wounds and illnesses. Seppo, the artist, painted pictures of our oppressing hostage life. My father kept a diary. Sonja organized food. And we all wrote pleading letters to our embassies and gave interviews to advance negotiations through media pressure.

But some of us remained stuck in our helpless fear, including my mother. Only very rarely she managed to call up what previously had given her great strength—helping others and encouraging people. She was like that when my father suffered from pancreatitis—then she returned to her old self again. But mostly it was a role swap, it was my father and me helping her to deal with the daily challenges and to survive critical situations. It was very demanding, but by doing it, we gained some strength in return. More important was that helping reduced our own fears.

Helping Others Is Helping Yourself

Sometimes I get asked what we did all day and whether it was quite boring. We didn't have any "responsibilities," but there was always a lot to do. Small everyday duties became a veritable challenge in the rainforest: bodily hygiene without running water, washing in the river (if there was one), preparing food (if we had some), cleaning and tidying (without a mop in a bamboo hut with a muddy floor)—those are only a few examples. What is already tedious in everyday life, in the jungle was ten times as bad. During the time when my mother couldn't walk, this effort was a hundred times as hard. It was never boring; no, in fact it was very demanding. But it had one advantage: with all those tasks we didn't have much time to dwell on our situation.

Assuming the role of helper in a crisis doesn't only give you strength but also courage, particularly in a life-threatening situation. This phenomenon I only really understood after our release when I saw a video clip of us in the jungle. The first Philippine TV station camera team that visited us arrived at the very moment when we were fleeing the military for a second time. We were crouching behind some bushes, my mother between us on a makeshift stretcher. She couldn't walk, was dehydrated, semiconscious, and had recently needed to be ventilated. Marie put a calming hand on her back, I fanned some air in her direction, and father appealed in front of the camera to the Philippine government.

Then, suddenly, there were rifle salvoes from the "front." At this point, the Philippine military was our enemy. Most of the hostages crouched deeper into the bushes, which was the only thing they could do in this situation. I kept upright, in seemingly stoic calmness, and continued to fan air toward my mother. In hindsight, that was quite reckless. When we watched this clip later, back in freedom, my father asked why I hadn't ducked down. Only then I realized that at the time I feared more for my mother than for myself.

When the camera team had gone, we continued to flee. Four people put the stretcher with my mother on their shoulders and ran for their lives. When the artillery shots were whizzing closer, the rebels shouted, "Drop! Drop!" and we hastily and carefully ducked down on the ground with the stretcher. When the detonations were over, we put the stretcher on our shoulders again and ran on. It was a scene I had only seen before in war movies. Was it heroic, do you think? No, it wasn't. At that moment, I only concentrated on my mother not falling off the stretcher. That was more important to me than the fear of being hit by a bullet. I felt lucky to be able to help. It gave me strength and took away the fear.

Other hostages described later how much it had helped them to help others. Marie, for example, was at her very best when she tended the bullet wounds of the rebels or helped my mother by administering mouth-to-mouth resuscitation.

Helping helps in a crisis. Helping others means helping oneself. It can be observed in many emergencies, for example, when a house is on fire. Many people panic and are full of fear. But in most cases, there is someone who remains absolutely calm and directs the traffic. This person senses their own strength and is a calming influence on others. They are focused on helping, while their own fear fades into the background. Assuming the role of helper provides a great chance and helps you to deal with a crisis. But it also contains a risk when one doesn't recognize one's own limitations.

First Help Yourself, Then Others

To sacrifice oneself seems like a heroic act, but sometimes it is reckless or even irresponsible. My father once had acted selflessly when he gave his drinking water to my mother, instead of seeing to it that he himself was hydrated enough. He stopped washing his hands, to save water, and sustained a bad infection on his finger leading to a high temperature and collapse. In the end, he was helping no one, because he wasn't available anymore as a helper and now needed support himself. "Well meant doesn't always mean well done."

Helping others at the cost of neglecting oneself or for a heroic death is no good for anyone. You can only help others when you first see to your own basic needs. The safety announcements on every flight tell you: "When the oxygen masks drop from above your head, pull it toward you and place it over your nose and mouth. Only then help children and other vulnerable persons to put their mask on."

I've always been annoyed by this announcement.

Intuitively, one would think that helping children and other vulnerable people first would be the right thing to do. But in that situation too it's vital to "keep your head!" Helpers must first make sure whether they can be of help at all. In case of a traffic accident, the rule is that, before the first responder can assess the situation, they have to make themselves safe, park their own car at a safe distance, switch on the hazard light, and put on the safety vest. It might sound egocentric to first look after your own safety, but it makes sense. It makes sense for doting parents who need some downtime, or employees who need a holiday. But in everyday life, it's not very popular. Colleagues who are always available and ready to take on every burden, according to the mantra "someone has to do it" are definitely more popular. This type of person, I call the "heroes of the workplace." They gain strength from the (presumed) selfless helping and quite often go under with it. Good executives see that their colleagues and employees will look after themselves enough. I've been in both situations and learned a lot from it.

Inspiration for the Protective Factor "Self-Efficacy"

The sense of impacting your own destiny gives great strength, especially in a crisis. It keeps us from sliding into the role of a victim and consequently feeling a sense of helplessness. Being active in a difficult situation reduces anxiety. Everyone has their own way of being effective, has a talent or an interest. It's a good thing to know your resources and to use them consciously. I personally have found helping very constructive. But you also must look after yourself in order to stay strong. When in doubt, first help yourself, even though it might feel difficult sometimes.

Never Walk Alone!

From the beginning, we had the rule amongst us to protect each other from attacks, especially the women. "Never walk alone!" was our mantra.

Patrick, the Filipino hostage, had warned us, "Don't ever allow, if at all possible, one of you to leave the camp with one of the rebels. Sometimes the hostage gets beaten up or assaulted, so that they will send a suitably dramatic appeal by phone to the outside world."

From the beginning, we only went to the toilet or to have a wash in the river accompanied by another hostage, and one of them had to be a man. Marie, who had been traveling on her own, had told the kidnappers right from the start that I was her fiancé to protect herself. We played the roles very convincingly—which wasn't difficult because we liked each other.

Together Through the Crisis

I felt hugely lucky not to have been abducted on my own. A group gives you strength. Apart from that, our group mainly consisted of couples, and couples give each other support and through that also to the group. Our family worked well together, but with a different pattern than in my childhood, because my mother had swapped her role as a helper to one of being helped. The hostage group was a social network that carried us through, and, as in my mother's case, also literally.

Neighborhood help in day-to-day life is always a great support. You help each other, tackle things together, watch out for of each other, and provide—when it's going well—a sense of safety. In our fast-moving times, the social integration in a neighborhood and larger families gets lost more and more and is replaced by social networks, mostly the digital ones. In that sense, we had an invaluable advantage on Jolo. We were in an analog world and immediate neighbors, living together in one place without walls or doors. If someone wasn't well, it was noticed straightaway. We comforted each other, encouraged each other, or bitched about each other—at times—because a shared sorrow is half a sorrow.

There were also moments of togetherness when we distracted ourselves with games, for example with our "Happy Hostage Game" (watch out—black humor!). I had painted a kind of Ludo pattern on a piece of wood, and Stéphane had sculpted the pieces and dice out of bamboo. The aim of the game was to gain freedom and to overcome obstacles, such as "Careful! Military Attack! Stay put for the next round!" People on the outside might have found this game rather irritating, but in our involuntary self-help group, we shared the same fate and fully understood the situation of the others.

The close community was definitely supportive, mentally as well as practically. But just as in real life, neighbors can also get on your nerves. Conclusively, one could say that the life of a lonely fighter is maybe less complicated, but living in a community is definitely easier. There's an African proverb: "If you want to travel fast, walk alone. If want to travel far, walk with others."

In a sense, our kidnappers belonged to our community as well, but at more of a distance. At the end of the day, they would always be our enemies, but in day-to-day life they often supported us. We asked them for help when we couldn't manage on our own, like when we needed a sharp knife for cutting banana leaves for making rain shelters. We asked them for advice in dealing with poisonous insects, for someone to help with getting the water from the river, and many more things. They were used to life in the jungle and knew a lot of tricks. What do you use in the jungle to clean your teeth? Many fighters always carried a machete. Among other things, they used it to cut, from the bark of a coco palm, a strip one centimeter wide and ten centimeters long. On the inside it was fibrous, and during the first days we used it as a rudimentary toothbrush—of course, without toothpaste.

It also helped to establish a good relationship with at least one of the rebels. To greet them in a friendly way was just as good manners as in Europe, even though the greeting rituals were different here. If a rebel liked you, they would press their thumb on yours and make a turning movement. They liked it when we took this up. Jokes were popular as well, but due to their limited knowledge of English, these jokes were restricted to one-word sentences. For example, I showed them the long scar on my arm from a lift accident when I was a child. I pointed to it and said, "fighting." Two reactions were possible now: the rebels would be filled with awe because scars were an evidence for courage, or they would see the joke in it and laugh. Both were good for the relationship.

Networking played an equally important role as at home, even though it was not among friends and colleagues. The rules were the same, though. Relationships were based on trust, created by alternate giving and receiving, and they took time to develop. From the start, we attempted to have a good relationship with our captors, which wasn't always easy, but was important for our survival, as we would find out later.

Support from the Outside

Just as important as the solidarity within the group was the contact with the outside world. Knowing that we weren't forgotten was incredibly helpful. German journalists supplied us with aid, letters, and news from home. Many people followed our fate in the media, got involved, and wrote letters. Complete strangers sent us parcels and letters. I was given a little ceramic bowl for foaming up shaving soap that a lady had made herself, together with a fine shaving brush made of badger hair. She had probably seen pictures of we bearded men in the jungle and thought that we could all do with a decent shave. Whether or not to shave wasn't our biggest problem, but the idea that somewhere in Germany someone was thinking of our wellbeing, and then made a little parcel and sent it to us moved me to tears. To this day I have that little ceramic bowl.

Contact with our friends and relatives at home was especially moving. We exchanged many letters, a contact organized by the embassy and carried out via journalists and messengers. Mail from home was as important for us mentally as water was for us physically. I was reminded of my grandfather, who had once told me how much strength he had gained from the letters his wife had sent him to the front, when he was a soldier in the Second World War. Mail from home strengthened the troops then, and we felt it in the same way.

My brother Dirk sent us a few very special aid parcels. They contained things we needed and had told the embassy about, such as special medication, decent sandals in the right size, our favorite crackers, and many more items. It helped tremendously. Even more important were his letters, which told us how much he was working for our release and what kind of a political and diplomatic apparatus had been set in motion for us. To have that help in the background was like fire cover from above. Just to know it was incredibly important.

Marie told us a very touching example about how her family helped and supported her. After a lengthy trek, she was completely exhausted and so low that she said, "I can't go on, and I don't want to go on anymore." A short time later, she heard the voice of her eighty-year-old father on one of the rebel's radios. He was directly addressing her. "Marie, if you hear me, I'm here …" He had flown to Manila to wait for his daughter. For Marie, it was the turning point. Her energy and her will to live returned.

The support from home was tremendous and helped us mentally as well as physically to the extreme. Knowing that other people prayed for our release gave us the hope that apart from outside help we would also get help from "above."

Inspiration for the Protective Factor "Social Support"

Social support works like a shield against stress, as it can weaken negative consequences of stress or even prevent them. According to the "Model for Processing Stress" by Lazarus (1984), it's a valuable resource because stressors are judged as less threatening. This was evidenced in laboratory studies (Ditzen, Heinrichs, 2007). They showed that social support clearly reduces physical responses to stress. The reason is oxytocin, a relational hormone that is released during social interactions and reduces the level of cortisol (a stress hormone).

The significance of a social network cannot be valued highly enough. For that reason, it's important to look after relationships and to foster social networks—but *before* an emergency. Only then are you able to get help from the social network in a crisis instead of remaining a lone wolf facing difficult situations.

Keep It Up!

In situations that deplete you of strength and undermine your principles, it's especially difficult not to get sloppy, but very important to keep up standards. Everyone knows this: The more stressed you are, the weaker you feel; the more you would like to indulge yourself or just lounge around. In the jungle it was like this:

"I'll throw the leftover food under the platform, instead of carrying it into the woods in the pouring rain. It's all a bit much here anyway ..." The consequences were clear: The rotting food attracted insects and mice.

"I find it too difficult to stand at the trickle of a spring for ten minutes and be eaten alive by mosquitoes, until the coconut shell is filled with water. I just won't wash my hands today." As a consequence, many suffered serious infections and itchy skin diseases.

"It's raining and it's dark ... I'll do my business nearby instead of going further into the woods." If you then stepped into the shit barefooted you got a worm infection—it could have been avoided.

Our life in the jungle was challenging physically as well as mentally—day after day. To survive, we needed constant discipline. That concerned our hygiene, no matter how demanding it was to get to a water source. If we could bathe in a river or have a shower under a waterfall, we always took the opportunity to wash our clothes as well. Apart from personal hygiene, physical fitness was also very important to be able to endure the hardships in the long run.

Fitness for the Future

At the beginning of our "adventure," we had all been reasonably fit. As divers, we were used to keeping in good physical condition. But the meager rations of rice and water on Jolo depleted us, and we all lost weight. I shed about ten kilograms, others considerably more. Monique joked that the rebels were the most effective weight watchers she'd ever seen. Hunger increased our exhaustion, but also prompted more gallows humor. Doing exercises here was not an option. But each aid packet improved our situation noticeably.

After a few weeks, we could all eat as much as we wanted because we had received a large number of battle rations from the *Bundeswehr* (the German armed forces). Unfortunately, the meals were all the same: Type 3B meatballs in tomato sauce. Even after the twentieth portion, we would just devour them anyway. In the last camp, where I spent nearly three months, the food was more varied, and there was always enough water.

Some among us never stopped eating and used food as a distraction, even though the situation was just as threatening as before. That was risky, because at any moment there could have been another attack by the military, followed by a long exhausting trek to escape it. It would have made sense to prepare for this mentally *and* physically. But those people were optimists—and this time they were right to be. At our release, they were comparatively well-nourished.

Others made use of the better supply of nourishment to do exercises, possibly to prepare themselves for a long and arduous captivity. My father walked a certain distance each day in a pair of wellies he had received in one of the aid packages. They were not exactly what you needed in the jungle, but it helped to increase his stamina.

My fitness program was a daily routine of three times thirty push-ups, squats, and sit-ups, as well as weightlifting with a gallon bottle of water. I didn't only do it out of boredom or for fun, but to also prevent my muscles from becoming flabby in the difficult conditions.

Toward the end of our "jungle camp," Stéphane constructed a bamboo fitness trail in the forest where we could practice pull-ups and stretching. This was more for fun but also gave us a feeling of usefulness. Its construction was a kind of exercise too.

It took a lot of discipline to get going and work yourself into a sweat when the air was already very humid and hot, especially as you had to wash in the river afterwards, attacked by swarms of mosquitoes. But it was worth it because it made us all more balanced mentally. Exercise doesn't only strengthen the body but the mind too by releasing "happiness hormones." And it was about keeping up our standards in the literal, physical sense as well as metaphorically. As we sat on the ground most of the time, it easily promoted a feeling of subjugation.

The effect of body posture on the mind has been proven by several scientific studies. To reduce stress, it is recommended to take on a so-called power posture: standing with your legs spread out, arms raised in a gesture of enthusiasm. After two minutes, the level of the stress hormone cortisol drops noticeably. I didn't know this at the time, but intuitively did exactly that, and I always felt the benefit. I really recommend it when you're under stress—not only in the jungle.

Forest Bathing

Shinrin Yoku is a Japanese method for stress reduction. It means "forest bathing." The act of consciously engaging with a forest environment is becoming more and more popular in Europe, because it has such a beneficial effect on health and wellbeing. The mere sight of a forest is said to reduce stress hormones, lift the spirit, and balance the mind.

I can confirm this, even now in my European environment. I love the woods and even after a short walk, always feel refreshed and invigorated.

As hostages in precarious conditions, we developed a love-hate relationship with the rainforest. But it was beneficial to our mental and physical wellbeing to be outside day and night and exposed to a lot of sunlight. In any case, we were in an environment that could only inspire and build our resilience.

The three most important forms of resilience were stated by Lepore and Stevens. They use a vivid example of a tree exposed to a storm. The first form of resilience is that of *resistance,* such as when a massive tree withstands a storm without moving. The second form is *regeneration.* The tree flexes with the wind and afterwards returns to being upright. The third form, *reconfiguration,* describes another way of dealing with stress: the tree changes its direction of growth in order to offer less resistance to a future storm.

In my own life, I have learned how important reconfiguration can be—to reorientate after a storm, rather than just to withstand it or simply stand up again afterwards. It's a completely different challenge: to get through a crisis with strength and to be stronger as a result of it.

During our captivity, we were first challenged to meet the external stress with resistance (steadfastness) and regeneration (flexibility). On Jolo, we had very inspiring role models for that.

I was endlessly impressed by the rainforest capacity to regenerate. After about three months, and accompanied by some of the rebels, I went back to the first camp from which we had fled after coming under attack. The roof of our bamboo hut was riddled with bullet holes. Apart from that, nature had reconquered the entire space. What we had left behind had been a scene of devastation. The paths were well-trodden because we had used the nearby bushes as our latrine. All around it the banana leaves had been cut back because hundreds of rebels had used them for shelter from the rain, as sleeping mats, or even plates. The bamboo bushes had been hacked down, mostly for building huts. But no trace of that was left. Nature was definitely winning. Bamboo stalks are really blades—the plant is a kind of grass. They can grow as high as thirty meters and grow half a meter a day. They are stable and flexible at the same time. In a storm, they bend with the wind and afterwards straighten up again. Because of its regenerative resistance, bamboo is an excellent symbol for resilience.

The quick transition from life to death was part of our natural environment. We found vivid examples in the animal world. One morning, I found a giant dead lizard by the path. By the evening, all that was left was its skeleton, cleaned by an army of ants that were carrying away the last fibers of its flesh. It was an impressive example for how fleeting and transient life in this environment was. We had to come to terms with these ever-changing circumstances and the fact that at no time did we know for certain what turns our hostage drama would take. Orderliness and tidiness played a central role for our survival.

Order in Order to Survive

In our previous normal day-to-day life and work, we were used to planning, organizing, and making decisions. In the jungle, we were dependent on the volatility of our captors and the rhythms of nature, even in our basic needs. One event followed another—military attacks, exhausting treks, rain, visiting journalists, hut building, and so on. The harder the burdens were, the stronger our desire to simply crash out, just have some downtime. In the first few days, we dropped down exhausted on the empty rice bags in the sleeping quarters to somehow process the events of the day. Then suddenly the sun went down, and it was pitch black around us. We didn't have any flashlights, so we had to feel our way in the dark. Half blind, we stumbled through the night on treacherous paths to find a place in the stinking bushes to relieve ourselves. You could never see whether the "toilet" had been used by someone before. And the search for leaves to use as toilet paper was quite difficult too. Once I tore off a limp banana leaf, and suddenly felt hundreds of ants crawling up my arm. This taught me the value of sticking to orderliness and discipline. The entry in my diary from that time says, "Important: maximal organization with minimal energy!"

My brother would probably never have experienced such troubles. He had learned his lesson in the army. Soldiers are drilled to routinely store their equipment tidily in their locker and fold their clothes with mathematical precision. What had appeared to me as pointless affectation before now made sense. In an emergency, soldiers have to get dressed quickly and find their clothes in the dark. The same routine makes working in some civil workplaces easier too, for example, in a workshop or office. When you need something urgently, you have to respond quickly and cannot afford to lose time searching for things. Blessed are those who can stick to a well-structured system, be it in the toolbox, in the filing cabinet, or on the hard drive. The more chaotic things are around you, the more discipline you need to keep order, even when it seems difficult.

We stuck to that principle in the jungle too—at least some of us. Eventually we set up a structured daily routine, ruled by the sun. In the mornings, we fetched water, if that was possible. During the day, we organized our things and made a pile of leaves in a specific place for the night-time toilet tour. Before sunset, we conducted our big hygiene session. That all worked quite well during the quieter phases. After demanding events, such as a day-long trek to a new hideaway, the system mostly collapsed. Or rather, *we* collapsed—with exhaustion.

After a crisis, chilling out is a great temptation. You want to recover from the stressful day. It's perfectly human and sometimes an important first step. But in the long run, the next dangerous event is lurking in the comfort zone. Because *after* the last crisis is always also *before* the next crisis. It's vitally important to prepare for the future and learn from the mistakes and insights of the past crisis, as long as we remember it. Otherwise there's the danger of making the same mistakes again and again.

Exactly that has happened to me after our release. I was so euphoric about my newly found freedom that I lost my head and returned to my old comfort zone. What happened then was probably the most painful lesson of my whole life.

Inspiration for the Protective Factor "Fitness and Discipline"

In a stressful situation, it's particularly important not to let yourself down. To overcome your inner sloth, you need discipline. You can train it by, for example, taking a cold shower each morning. That truly rips you out of your comfort zone and increases your energy level. Forest bathing or jogging around your workplace during your lunch break increases mental and physical fitness. There might not be time during hectic periods of your life, but you have to be aware of that too. That is also a question of discipline.

STRONGER THROUGH A CRISIS

Back to the Comfort Zone

People who heard about my time as a hostage typically made two assumptions about my life afterwards that couldn't differ more. Some assumed that the traumatic experience would be a burden for me forever—baggage to carry around. Others thought that after such an extreme experience nothing in "normal" life could ever stress me again—that I would resurface in a kind of enlightened state of mind. Neither is the case.

Fortunately, I survived the kidnapping unharmed. The protective factors of resilience helped me to remain strong during those stressful times. The extreme experience didn't destroy me, but it didn't make me immune to stress either, as many seemed to believe. Quite honestly, I had believed this myself while still in the jungle. If I survive this, I used to think, then the more trivial everyday worries such as deadlines at work will never stress me again. After all, those "deadlines" aren't life-threatening, not like being kidnapped for a ransom that nearly had cost me my head. But everything turned out completely differently. A few years after my abduction, I suffered from burnout.

What had gone wrong? In hindsight, I realized that using one's strength to get through a crisis doesn't necessarily mean one comes out stronger. I came to this insight after an intensive search for evidence. I examined my previous life and focused on the decisive moments, the crises, and the watersheds. I found that, while dealing with a crisis, I had been making the wrong assumptions. I thought that a crisis is simply a hurdle you must overcome as quickly as possible. Afterwards, you would get up, dust yourself off, and get back in the saddle. That's exactly what I did after the kidnapping. I went back to my old life instead of taking the hint that fate had dropped in the form of my kidnapping experience.

Terror and Ending

On the morning of September 9, 2000, I had no idea that my release was imminent. We suddenly heard a massive amount of gunfire in the jungle. Again, we had to flee without knowing where to and from what. By now, there were only four Western hostages left: Seppo, Risto, Stéphane, and me. The others had been released already, apart from our Filipino mate Abi who was being kept in a different place.

After a hike of several kilometers, on the orders of Commander Robot, we climbed into a small treehouse in the middle of a clearing. We crouched down as we waited, extremely nervous as the shooting came closer and closer. Eventually, several military jeeps and other transport vehicles arrived. Two envoys from the Philippine negotiating team got out and began a heated discussion with Commander Robot. Apparently, they had the ransom money for our release. Their convoy had been shot at by a rival faction of Abu Sayyaf that feared for their share of the ransom money and tried to sabotage our release. There had been casualties and injuries among the envoys' bodyguards. What followed now was a nerve-racking haggling about us, which went on in front of us, with unmistakable body language. The envoys pointed to us and gestured with four fingers. Commander Robot raised three fingers and pointed to Seppo, Risto, and Stéphane. He only wanted to release three hostages. And of all things, it was me he wanted to keep as a bargaining chip to be safe from the Philippine military. Perhaps he also wanted more ransom money.

It was a cruel twist of fate that in the chaos of our release, I became the most important asset in the negotiations. I dreaded the prospect of remaining as the only one—no one else there to share my fate. Who could I talk to, who could I look after?

The shooting seemed to come closer. Time was running out. All of a sudden, the envoys, sweating with stress, shook hands with Commander Robot. He had agreed. My heart nearly stood still. Then came the liberating news: all four hostages would be set free!

We were told to climb on to the loading bed of one of the vehicles. Crammed together, we sat between heavily armed rebels and the envoys' bodyguards. The transport vehicle that had been attacked on the way had been used for moving the dead and injured soldiers. Our vehicle was open-sided and didn't offer any protection. Through the back opening, I could see more transport vehicles, crammed full of rebels, their weapons in position. Together with the rebels, we drove over a bumpy track for what felt like an eternity until we stopped at a tarmac road. The rebels jumped off, and soldiers of the Philippine army got in. That was a good sign. But I still tried not to be too euphoric. Always keep your head!

After a few kilometers on that road, we stopped by a field. Military helicopters were waiting for us. We lifted off toward freedom. The doors of the helicopter were removed, and armed soldiers were keeping watch below.

Looking at my friends, I was overwhelmed by an indescribable combination of feelings. They also didn't know whether to cry or to laugh. But then one last doubt crossed my mind: what if a surface-to-air rocket hit us? But after a journey that again seemed to last an eternity, we landed in safety. I saw the first solid houses for a long time, and dozens of people expecting us. I couldn't believe my luck. I was free again!

Free and Not Free

Soon after the euphoric phase immediately following our liberation, we sobered up. I had to deal with my new captivity as a public personality. I know that the incredible media attention during our time as hostages contributed to the peaceful resolution, and to this day, I'm grateful that we were able to benefit from the media attention—in contrast to many other hostages. But it had its price. I had to pay for it with my personal freedom.

It was not an option to simply fly home and rest. Public interest was huge, and the media pressure on the ex-hostages was relentless. After the people at home had feared for 'their' hostages for months and followed the events in the media, they wanted to know how the whole event had been for us. I took on the role as a public personality only reluctantly and felt just as overwhelmed and unprepared as I had twenty weeks earlier when I landed in the jungle.

Even before we got out of the helicopter, countless local journalists pushed their cameras and microphones on long telescopic arms into our faces and shouted the first questions over the noise of the still running rotors. "Marc, how do you feel?" In my euphoric mood, I shouted back, "Fucking great!"

I then saw the familiar faces of our negotiating team in the waiting crowd. They were very happy for us and led us through the throng to one of the houses. From there, we flew directly to a military base, where I was greeted by the German ambassador, an officer from the federal police, and a German doctor. At that moment, it became clear to me how many people had worked relentlessly for us to be released unharmed. I felt immense gratitude.

Still on the tarmac, I gave the first interviews to many more microphones and expressed my gratitude to all the people at home for their support during the last few months. In the airport building, a further press conference was arranged, with live reporting by CNN and the BBC. Then, on we went in a Hercules transport plane. There was another stop in the Philippine city of Zamboanga—and another siege by journalists. The German ambassador handed me his mobile phone saying that the German foreign minister Joschka Fischer wanted to talk to me. It was crazy! Then came the next international press conference. I was still wearing my tattered jungle clothes, and all I wanted was to take a shower, close a solid door behind me, and take a deep breath. But the representatives of German TV stations asked me for an interview for the evening news, saying, "The nation is waiting!"

Okay. I agreed to one more interview with four German TV stations that agreed to comply with my request to keep it short. Afterwards, I could enjoy the first moment of privacy for months. A police officer accompanied me to my hotel room and offered to stay outside or even in the room for my own safety. But I only wanted one thing—to be by myself. I discovered the small wonders of civilization as if for the first time. A sit-down toilet, running water, a soft bed with a duvet, air conditioning. I was completely overwhelmed by the level of comfort that I had always taken for granted before.

The next morning, I tried to take a walk in the hotel grounds to recover from the ordeal and to get a sense of my new freedom. But that didn't happen because the media interest was unabating. Some German journalists approached me, but I apologized and asked to have the morning off to catch my breath. But one of them very clearly indicated that I didn't have a choice if I was interested in a balanced report with decent photos. We agreed to an arranged shoot, showing me on my second day in freedom sitting at the breakfast table reading the newspaper. I followed the journalist's directives patiently—a role I wasn't used to.

Like my father, I was to make a stop in Libya on the way home to present myself to the press in gratitude. This might sound crazy, but the ransom had been paid by Libya. According to some press reports, it was one million dollars per hostage. The Libyan ex-ambassador to the Philippines had supported the negotiations with a lot of empathy. For that reason, I thought that a thank-you gesture to Saif al-Islam al-Gaddafi, Muammar al-Gaddafi's son, was appropriate, because his foundation had supplied the ransom money. The country had been boycotted by the international community since the Lockerbie air disaster in 1989. With this humanitarian engagement, Libya now wanted to get back on the international stage.

The biggest surprise was that my brother was waiting to meet me in Tripoli. At last I could do what I had longed for most fervently in the jungle—to hug him and thank him for his support during the past few months. He had even managed to smuggle a can of lager into the strictly non-alcoholic country. It was one of the loveliest moments after my release. But then I only wanted to get back to Germany, and so I missed the arrival of the German Foreign Secretary, who was also coming to Tripoli to thank Libya for their contribution.

Three days after my release, I landed in Hanover in a government airplane. I stepped down the gangway with my brother Dirk. My mother came running toward me, followed by my father. We hugged for a long time, but that was all we had time for. Still on the airfield, I gave another interview—my first in Germany—something that seemed to be becoming more routine now. Then we traveled by coach to Göttingen, accompanied by the Minister for Culture of Lower Saxony, representing the government. It soon became clear that this wasn't just one of his official commitments, but that he had taken a personal interest in my family, and so we enjoyed his company very much.

The press was waiting in front of my parents' house in

Göttingen. I gave my last statements of the day, and then the door closed behind my family and me.

At last we were reunited as a family, in freedom and without anyone else around. My mother was feeling much better by now. On the day of my return, my father shaved off the beard he had grown as a hostage and looked a different man. My brother was with us again—at last. They were incredibly moving, these first moments of being together.

And then we had a very simple but utterly delicious cold dinner. I couldn't get enough of the dark, wholesome bread, cheese, pickled gherkins—and a beer. Only after all this time in the jungle, far away, did I realize what home really meant to me: it's the place of childhood, of familiar things, of feeling safe. The cool, fresh autumn air, the familiar smell of my parents' house, the clean tap water, the German news program *Tagesschau* ("Daily News"), the garden with its fruit trees, the neighbors, the song of the blackbirds ... all that was stored deep inside me and firmly anchored me to this place. Home is more than just a building or an area. For me, it's the source of my strength.

In no time at all, I got accustomed again to the luxuries of civilization. But now I could also consciously appreciate two European achievements that had only been mere words before: peace and freedom. I was free to do whatever I wanted and wasn't in fear for my life anymore. How much I cherished that now!

I stayed at home for about two weeks, recharging my

batteries. I met old friends, went for walks, had meals with the family in our favorite Greek restaurant, and visited the World Expo in Hanover. Everything was nearly as before, only that on our return, several journalists were waiting for us at home. We met the press, and gave a final interview. Then it was time to return to Luxembourg.

Every Ending Contains a Beginning ...

Back in Luxembourg, I was glad there wasn't so much media interest and that I was mostly left in peace. I needed time to sort myself out—that's what I thought anyway. First of all, I needed to organize things, like reregistering my car, going through my mail, and retrieving my computer password, which I had completely forgotten. I also had to sort myself out emotionally. I didn't want to simply take up my old love affairs, I wanted to get used to my old environment first—as my environment had to get used to me again. It had been four and-a-half months, but it felt like lightyears of absence. I met up with friends and colleagues to tell them of my experience and to catch up with what had happened here in the meantime. Many good conversations helped me to process my ordeal and to return, step by step, to my old life.

My employer PwC kindly left the decision to me as to when and how I wanted to take on new projects—while continuing to pay my salary, which they had never stopped while I was away in the jungle. I very much appreciated their generosity!

My bosses also organized a psychotherapist who specialized in trauma and wanted to assess whether I was suffering from post-traumatic-stress disorder (PTSD) and, if so, to treat me. After a few sessions, we both came to the amazing conclusion that I had survived the kidnapping without any long-term mental impact. The only thing I suffered from in the first few weeks was nightmares of the armed skirmishes in the jungle, from which I would awaken in a sweat. But they too subsided eventually.

Mostly, I needed the free time to say thank you to the many people who had supported us during the kidnapping—those who had prayed or written letters, watered my plants, signed petitions for our release, and made any number of other helpful gestures. It turned into a real challenge to reply to the letters from all over the world, but it was also a positive one, because I felt I could give something back after I had been on the receiving end of so much help.

I also spent time to do what, on Jolo, had been my ultimate idea of freedom. I went to a café, had a cappuccino, read a newspaper, and listened to the music in the background. Still, for weeks I seemed to live in a bubble. Somehow, many things simply felt unreal. I wasn't a captive in the jungle anymore and was conscious that I had been given a new life. It was a second chance—something not many people get.

But when I anticipated going back to my old job, I had mixed feelings. On the one hand, I felt indebted to my employers because of all their support. On the other hand, it meant going back to a career that had cost me a few sleepless nights, even before the kidnapping. But I could not think of any alternatives. A return to the old situation would help me to simply get my feet back on the ground.

I returned to my old position as a consultant in financial projects. But I found it even harder than before to generate interest in the abstract issues of the finance world. My old dilemma—investment funds or private banking—was still looming. I didn't feel attracted to either of them. Again, I had to make a painful decision—but both meant pain. The clarity I had experienced during the kidnapping ("This is about my life!") had vanished. But my old life didn't offer any normality either. The label "ex-hostage" was too prominent. I couldn't simply have normal financial discussions with my clients. It wasn't "business as usual." Often, my clients were dying to ask me questions about the kidnapping.

It was impossible to return to the role of a consultant with this in the background. The following example illustrates the dilemma. Dressed as usual in a dark, smart suit, I was in a lift, together with clients and colleagues, when a woman came in. She looked at me, recognized me, and shouted: "Oh, God, the jungle man!" This made it clear to me that neither I nor my workplace could return to the way things were before.

After my existential experience in the jungle, I had even less interest in the analyses of calculations and financial projections. But I didn't have a clue of what I could do instead. Somehow, it felt like I had been given a free pass. I thought that everyone would understand and later forgive me if I took some time out from my career. I had also realized that I wasn't irreplaceable—something I had previously had the arrogance to assume. My projects had been taken over by colleagues without any hiccups.

During my captivity, I had wondered about doing something I would enjoy or that made sense in my "second life." But the only thing I had come up with was "to play the piano in a bar"—that had been on my bucket list in my jungle diary. One of my favorite films is "The Fabulous Baker Boys." Jeff Bridges is the embodiment of my romantic dream as a bar pianist. At one point, he expresses his feelings by tinkling along in a smoky pub, lost in deep thoughts. I always loved that scene.

As it happened, toward the end of the year 2000, I fell in love with a woman from Cologne. My feelings were very intense, like I had never felt before. One night, I Googled "music jazz Cologne" and found out that one could study jazz music at the Cologne College of Music. That was another sign! The very next morning, I went to my boss and announced, "I've fallen in love. I am moving to Cologne to study music."

Without a doubt, I was still on a high thanks to my newfound freedom. I took the liberty to do what I wanted to do—music. But the even stronger drive was love. I arrived in Cologne shortly afterwards, with butterflies in my stomach, and had the most wonderful time of my life with my girlfriend. She took some weeks off from the university, and we spent most of the time together. As a Northerner, I had to do a crash course in the eccentricities of the Cologne Carnival, but soon I loved the city and its happy-go-lucky people.

I also tried my luck as a musician. The idea was to earn money as a drummer, like before, and to study the piano. It was an old dream, and it seemed to be coming true.

I became the drummer in the cover band Ströhlein und Konsorten (Ströhlein and Company), run by the TV journalist Marcus Ströhlein, to this day my best friend. We recorded a CD and played some gigs in the area, one at a huge biker festival. It was great fun, but it wasn't enough to make a living.

My piano studies were short-lived. When I went to the conservatory, I realized that I didn't want to obtain another degree, particularly one that involved boring topics such as the history of music and theory of music. I only wanted to play the piano. So, I took private lessons with a jazz pianist, because so far, I had only played by ear. Reading music wasn't my thing, and I was too lazy to seriously engage with it. Apart from that, compared with my highly motivated and qualified competitors, I was a bit too old. And as a musician with only modest talent, nobody gave me the praise I wanted. I was okay as an amateur musician, but felt embarrassed to say "I'm a musician" if someone asked me what I did. I definitely wasn't good enough to be a pro. What had I been imagining? Definitely not a life as a musician on the brink of poverty.

My savings dwindled as there was hardly any money coming in. Without a proper job and no money, I gradually turned from a jungle hero into an unemployed person in an existential crisis. This wasn't good for my relationship either, because my girlfriend was now embarking on her career at full speed. The sense of a "lightness of being" vanished, and the old lack of direction returned. Again, I found it difficult to make a decision and to take charge of my life. I missed the clarity I had felt in the Philippines when constantly facing death. Whatever I had learned from my experience of being kidnapped couldn't be transferred easily to my actual life, as I had previously believed.

Inspiration

After a crisis, it's good to regain energy and confidence in a comfort zone, doing things that are fun and that give you strength. But I wish someone had also given me the following advice then: one should also try to process one's experiences intensely and to learn from them.

The Carousel of Crises Keeps on Turning ...

After my release, I got lost in the euphoria of my regained freedom. On the one hand, it was healthy to give myself time after the extreme experiences to recharge my batteries, to follow the call of love to Cologne, and to try out my dream of becoming a musician. On the other hand, I missed the chance to really learn from my experience and to grow personally. In my euphoric state, I lost my head. In hindsight, I should have thought about what fate's hint had meant. After all, my time in the jungle had given me plenty of indications about what gave me clarity and strength. But I only found the pearl of wisdom much later. It is human and at the same time futile to think about how much easier my life could have been if I had learned my lesson earlier.

After the euphoric state subsided, I landed back in the real world. My savings were gone, my professional confidence was at rock bottom, my relationship had become difficult. I had to do something urgently to get a grip on my life. And out of the blue came a tempting opportunity.

A Tempting Offer

My former boss in Luxembourg was planning to open an academy for German banks in Luxembourg that offered courses in professional development. He asked me whether I could see myself running training courses in intercultural communication. I immediately liked the idea, as I had a lot of experience in the field. During my time in college, I worked for the worldwide student organization AIESEC, placing students on internships abroad, preparing applicants for their stays of several months, and training them in international culture. My own experience abroad—as a student and while working—qualified me for the position, as well as my empathy and my multilingual skills. There was also my experience in the jungle, where I worked with other hostages of several nationalities and had to communicate with our Asian kidnappers.

I carried on with my music, but also concentrated on my work as a freelance trainer for more than a year. Nothing much came of the Luxembourg courses, but through my contacts with old student friends, I secured some commissions in Germany. In hindsight, I can say that I achieved quite a bit during a short amount of time.

At first, I ran courses in intercultural management. Then I received inquiries about training in conducting presentations and public speaking. At one point, I stood in for a professor and gave lectures on topics I didn't know that much about, such as staff management and marketing.

I enjoyed planning the courses and teaching people. But here, too, there was no quick financial success. The topics were also not the kind of thing I wanted to focus on in the long run. My kidnapping experiences were again a distraction. As soon as the participants asked questions, it became clear they were more interested in my personal history. Often, the first question was, "Were you tortured?" I realized very quickly that I didn't simply want to tell them an exciting story to satisfy their sensationalism. If I wanted to talk about my time in the jungle, it was to tell them what I learned from it.

But at the time, I wasn't able to rationalize the way in which the kidnapping had enriched my life and how I could make the experience valuable for other people as well. I should have grappled more intensely with the deeper meaning behind this extreme phase in my life. Maybe then I would have better understood fate's hint. I'm strong in issues that are close to my heart.

For two years, I tried to reorganize my life as a musician and a trainer. I enjoyed both roles, but I didn't feel fulfilled. Besides, I didn't earn enough money to make a living. I was without direction and under financial pressure—and urgently needed a clean break.

Repeating Mistakes

In desperation, I made a huge mistake: I tried to go back to my old life. The answer seemed to be to look for a job like the one in Luxembourg. With my international education and experience as a consultant with PwC, I would easily find a well-paid and secure job again. At least, that's what I thought ...

At the beginning of 2003, I started to apply for suitable positions. The labor market at the time was difficult, but I made a good start by being invited to two interviews—after only two applications. The first company decided to fill the position with someone from its own ranks. The other, a management consultancy, was quite a disappointment. I spent two days in their assessment center and got very good results, but in the final interview they told me: "Impressive résumé! And your ability to endure stress is remarkable. There's really nothing that would unsettle you. But after your trauma, you'd do better to process your experience and not come to work in such a stressful environment as management consultancy."

Typical, I thought—for Germany. In the United States, people are appreciated when they have overcome a crisis. Learning from mistakes is an important part of the culture in the corporate world. In the jungle, battle scars were considered a sign of experience rather than a stigma. Commander Robot repeatedly showed everyone all his scars and was admired for them. I was deeply disappointed by the rejection. I then tried a sweeping attack and wrote countless job applications. But they were all rejected. I was at a complete loss. I applied three times for a job with Renault, a car company near Cologne, the last time for a trainee position in the hope of at least getting to the interview stage. When I was rejected even for that, I plucked up the courage to call human resources to ask for the reason for my rejection. "What criteria for the traineeship don't I meet? I have two master's degrees and experience as a consultant. I'm fluent in English and French." The woman at the other end said she would investigate.

Then it all happened very quickly. To my amazement, I got an invitation for an interview the same day for a position in aftersales marketing. The interview was on a Friday. My future boss and I quickly worked out everything. Within hours, I went through all the necessary stages and was set to start the following Monday. I had been catapulted back to the fast lane.

On the first day, I realized almost immediately that I was again in the position of a firefighter. I was to lead a huge project dealing with the reorganization of the spare part network for German Renault dealers. The delivery of parts to more than one hundred Renault workshops had to be reorganized within the current year. There were only five calendar months left.

Some of the board members considered the project to be extremely complex and not really achievable in such a short time. But my immediate boss was convinced. "It's possible! It has to be! You can do it!" After a long period without any external recognition, it felt good that someone believed in me. It was like an injection of energy that sped me from zero to one hundred. For some reason, I was also reassured by the fact that the chances of the project's success were considered very small. It meant that I would always be able to meet expectations, and in my mind that was a good starting point. We got the project going. Within a very short time, I had a team of fifteen managers and experts from very different areas—from distribution, logistics, IT, marketing, and training to the legal department. My boss supported me in every way; he was enormously assertive from his position of authority. Also, right from the beginning he had bragged that I was his "super weapon."

The project was highly complex. In a very short time, we had to adapt IT systems, create storage capacities, devise contracts and put them in place, plan delivery routes, and negotiate with the dealers. There were hundreds of members of staff to train—within the company and in the dealer network—and many, many more issues. My project meetings soon became notorious because of their meticulous preparation and follow-ups. An enormous project blueprint listed all the necessary activities and responsibilities, all labeled with symbols of their present status in a traffic light system. Green stood for *done,* yellow for *in progress,* and red for *critical.* No team member wanted to see the red sticker, because this project involved millions, and the board was regularly informed about its progress. Because of its huge economical and legal implications, it was widely discussed in the company as well as within the dealer network. The preparations continued at a breakneck pace until the end of the year. On the day of the deadline, January 1, 2004, the restructuring of the dealer network was set to go live. We held our breath. On January 2, it was clear: the transition had been successful and unexpectedly smooth. Now I could happily enjoy general recognition. Everyone was full of praise. I was very relieved and proud and enjoyed my new status as a super manager, able to solve the most difficult problems.

My boss already envisaged me on a steep career trajectory, right up to the top. But I felt the first signs of burnout. Again, I had turned into a mercenary. I didn't feel fulfilled and didn't see any deeper meaning in what I was doing. But my job had taken over everything, so I never had any time to reflect on it.

I'd never thought that I would ever again allow myself to be stressed out by something like a deadline. But I had gotten used to my comfortable lifestyle again all too quickly. I was on the hamster wheel chasing money and recognition again.

The next project, *Grosshandelsfunktion* (wholesale management) was even harder. It had already caused three former project managers to throw in the towel. The name alone made everyone shudder. But my boss was convinced. "It'll work out! It has to! You can do it!" And so, I again applied myself to a job that was about as close to my heart as the price of a pound of sugar. I couldn't care less where Renault got its parts from. Economically it made sense, but in the end no individual would be better or worse off. At least, that's how I saw it.

I felt most fulfilled and motivated when colleagues personally turned to me for help—asking for feedback about a critical email, searching for some vital information, or simply seeking a sympathetic ear when they needed someone to talk to. I always took time for those things, because the way my colleagues looked up to me made me feel good. I was doing something that made immediate sense, and it gave me strength. But then I spent too much time on those voluntary side projects and neglected my real work. It was a dilemma. Should I do what I like even though it's time-consuming, or concentrate on my actual work, which demanded more and more of my energy?

The more pressure I was under from the big project, the more often I was forced to refuse helping my colleagues, and I found that difficult. Being helpful is very important to me. But reliability is equally important. I couldn't simply neglect my actual work. But whatever I did, I would disappoint someone or ignore one of my core values. This conflict caused me a lot of stress. Only later did I come across a technique to resolve such a dilemma in a supportive and effective way.

I wish I had been given the following advice back then. It's the wonderful "dilemma communication" model by

Gunther Schmidt, founder of the hypno-systemic approach. In my example, I could have told a colleague seeking help: "I have a dilemma here. Part of me wants to help you, but another part of me finds it very important to concentrate on my own project, especially as I'm under such a lot of pressure to deliver with a looming deadline." You express your conflict openly, involve the other party in your decision-making process, and strengthen the social bond. At the same time, this method of communication emphasizes the important decision to give priority to your own real issues.

The trust of my colleagues was like fuel for me. Even more important was the support and the recognition of my boss. For that, time and time again, I went to my limits and beyond. I slaved with the obsession of a dog fetching sticks, even when I was thrown a veritable tree trunk to fetch back from a swamp. But at the end of the day, it was the recognition that drove me and not an inner vision or a deep conviction. But all this stopped a short time later when the company's leadership changed.

I now had a new boss who couldn't support me, because he first had to find his own feet on the project. At the same time, a rather autocratic director took over the aftersales distribution department. She focused on me and pulled the plug on the unpopular project I was working on. She and my new boss were under a new executive from France who was extremely clever but also had to find his footing. So, things quickly went downhill for me. Instead of being driven by a wind from behind, it was blowing full into my face. I was fighting windmills. I knew it would end in burnout, but I kept on fighting. And my team was reduced, the expected results increased, the budget slashed. I tried in vain to remind my superiors of the previous, realistic targets that had been agreed to before the change of management, but no one listened. I submitted suggestions with detailed scenarios, but they were ignored. My new boss said something like, "We all have to recalibrate. Just carry on as before. We'll sort it out later."

Step by Step Toward a Burnout

I tried desperately to compensate for the missing team members while at the same time hitting the new targets. I made suggestions for prioritizing issues, but the decisions on them were constantly postponed.

But instead of accepting the consequences, I made even more of an effort and, driven by the fear of losing my job, increased my weekly hours from fifty to eighty, while constantly telling myself: "I mustn't lose my job, I can't disappoint my boss. I have to do what he says." Physically I was a free man, but mentally I felt like a hostage to my boss and my job. But at the end of the day, it was me holding myself hostage and I was incapable of freeing myself from the situation.

My life was spent at work and in bed, and I was ready

to combine the two to save on commuting time. No more hobbies, hardly any social contacts, breaks only when physically necessary. Instead, I drank more and more coffee to stay awake and downed a quick glass of wine in the evening to drop off more easily. Only on weekends did I have the space and time to work on a growing pile of other demands and tasks and catch up a bit. I don't have to spell it out that I had clearly crossed the border from a sustainable kind of life to rat-race country.

I lived on a hamster wheel, convinced that achievement was the only thing that counts in life. I wasn't living, I was merely existing. I ran faster and faster and never got anywhere. There was no end goal or opportunity to stop and rest. My situation felt hopeless. My reactions to the stress were sleeping problems, twitching eyelids, and permanent arrhythmia. Several times at night I woke up dripping with sweat and scribbled down things that seemed important for the next day. Sometimes I even smoked a cigarette in frustration and went straight back to the office in the morning. I felt that I was always on duty and couldn't switch off any more to recharge my batteries. Despite all this, I remained efficient for weeks and weeks and kept my reduced team going for an amazingly long period. But then came the day. Three or four colleagues stood in the doorway of my office and shouted: "Where are the figures?" "I sent you an email yesterday." "The meeting has started. Are you coming?"

Suddenly, I no longer knew what to do. It was like I was

having a blackout. Should I look at my emails? Or look for the table in Excel? Or go to the meeting? What meeting, actually? All I could hear was a rushing sound and echoing voices all at once. I froze. That's the moment when the "TILT!" sign lights up on a pinball machine. Nothing works anymore. Instinctively, I did the right thing, as it was the only option left to me. I pressed the off button on my computer and went home.

But not straightaway. First, I went to see my boss and said in so many words: "Sorry, find someone else for the job. Once I'm fit again, I'll help him or her find their feet. I'll be in touch." It felt as if an emergency system had taken over and switched me to autopilot. Part of me watched myself standing in front of my boss and with disbelief heard my own words. How could I say something like that? Did I know what I was doing? But it happened. It happened to me, the super manager for the most difficult problems.

And then I really went home. I don't remember how I got there. The first thing I can recall is that I lay on my bed as if turned into stone and listened to the roaring noise in my ears. Otherwise, there was stillness because I had switched off my phone. How long I remained like that and what I did then, I don't remember. At some point, it must have sunk in how critical my situation was.

I was completely exhausted, but I hardly slept over the following days. The whirlwind of thoughts in my head kept me awake, and I was overcome by a whole range of conflicting feelings. How could that have happened? I failed! How will the team get on without me? What are they thinking of me? Should I have continued somehow? Could I have prevented this? Was it my fault or was it the circumstances? I felt ashamed to have let my team down and to have failed, but on the other hand, I was relieved that the unrelenting stress was now over. Changes were long overdue in this muddled situation, but I hadn't managed to make a constructive decision or any adjustments.

In a difficult situation, such as a demanding job, there are usually three options: *leave it, love it, or change it*! The following questions should help you come to a decision:

1. *Leave it*: Do I want to leave the situation? How could I do that in practice? What legal, social, and financial consequences would it have? Is there an alternative? How quickly could I find a new direction? What would be the best time to extricate myself from the situation?
2. *Love it*: Can I learn to love the situation, and how? What advantages does my situation or my job have for me? What can I learn from it for later life? How can I deal with the situation better to be able to endure it? Could I take on the challenges in a less stressful way?
3. *Change it*: Can I change the situation or the job? What exactly would I change? What are the possibilities and limitations of making such changes?

> Who could help me? Who would be able to decide about the changes? How could I change in the situation? What would I have to learn?

I had been asking myself some of those questions for a while. *Leave it*? I had a well-paid job, even though the money more and more felt like compensation for pain. It wouldn't be easy to find a comparable position quickly. I also didn't have a clue what I would be looking for. I didn't have the time or the energy to even think about it.

Love it? The cooperation with my team was a very positive factor in this job. But the constant analyses and targets remained agonizing for me even though I tried very hard to come to grips with them. I couldn't find a deeper meaning in my work, some human connection. I tried hard to generate some enthusiasm for the world of cars, but, as opposed to many of my colleagues, I wasn't a petrol head.

Change it? My attempts to change my job situation had failed. Additional support for the mathematical side, the analyses, had been rejected. My team had even been reduced. The tasks should have been prioritized and allocated differently, but my proposals were never considered, and so I didn't manage to change anything. The decision-making process—*leave it, love it* or *change it*—had been long overdue, until my body and my mind eventually took over and said "leave it!"

After my breakdown, I suddenly had a lot more time to think. The slower the destructive carousel of my self-blaming thoughts turned, the more that constructive thoughts edged into the foreground. I reflected on my situation and how I got into it, remembering the many conversations I had had with friends and colleagues in the past few weeks. I realized that they had more or less entirely revolved around me and my dire situation. For ages, I hadn't had the time for relaxed chats or carefree social meetups. Also, I had felt less and less able to get involved with other people and their issues, something I had always been good at. My thoughts had only focused on me. I felt ashamed realizing it.

Had some of these conversations been constructive? It did help when the other person simply listened and let me talk. That worked like a safety valve to help release some of the pressure I was under. But people rarely just listened. Mostly they responded, sometimes in a helpful way, sometimes not. They offered pity and validation, advice and criticism, and some also gave honest and constructive feedback. Pity and emotional validation were what I'd mostly hoped for from my friends. But over time, it had turned me into a victim and stripped me of the motivation and strength to change anything about either myself or the situation. I felt confirmed as a victim of circumstance.

Equally unhelpful were the conversations full of simple advice. "Just grit your teeth and get through it!" or "Just take a few days off." This felt like someone hitting my bruised soul. I didn't feel that my agony was properly acknowledged; it felt like criticism. Two good friends helped me most when they gave me supportive, honest, and constructive feedback. They showed their understanding in the best possible way, were able to assess my situation, and showed compassion. But even they didn't meet my need for recognition and praise. For some reason, I felt harshly treated and wanted more empathy, but I also felt that they were seriously concerned. With best intentions, they asked unpleasant questions, such as "Why do you keep going when you know the job isn't right for you?" "Is it possible that you find it difficult to say *no* because you want to get it right for everybody?" "Do you think you could not be perfect, just for once?" Those were the right questions to make me focus on my blind spots. But I needed to burn out first to face those unpleasant truths.

For the first time in my life, I went to see a psychotherapist on my own initiative. It felt like declaring emotional bankruptcy. I was ashamed because I had to admit to myself that I had failed. But my therapist said it was the first step toward recovery. It would take a few weeks, and I would have to work on it so I wouldn't end up in the same situation again. To carry on would not be an option, and definitely not under the same working conditions as before. Session after session consolidated what I had guessed already after my friends' uncomfortable questions. The reasons for my collapse were mainly in me—not the conditions at work. Some personality traits I had always been proud of had apparently led to my downfall at work: perfectionism, ambition, involvement, striving for harmony. Those were my so-called inner drivers, the reasons I stayed on the hamster wheel until I collapsed. "You're not allowed to make any mistakes!" "Work harder! "You mustn't disappoint other people!" "If you don't get this done, there will be problems!"

I learned that if I kept following those voices from my childhood, I would again end up on the hamster wheel. I needed to set better boundaries and say *no* every now and then. Calls for help such as "We have to set priorities, otherwise we'll go under," would not be sufficient. I had to learn to ask for decisions early and pursue them consistently. And I had to say things like "I won't carry on unless we set priorities." That wasn't easy for me, but it promised more success in the long run.

After a few days of absence, I had a phone call from my boss's superior on the board. "I'm sorry. We didn't respond to your suggestions, and that was our mistake. We rely on you and hope that you'll be back soon. Until then, I'll see to it that the necessary changes will be adopted. Promise!"

It felt good to hear that. They persuaded me to come back to my old position after a few weeks and many therapy sessions. But I knew that there was more at the root of the crisis than a mistake by management. It was also my own mistake not to have set firmer boundaries at an earlier stage. I decided to give it a second chance.

After a few weeks, I went back to the office, at first for four, then six, then eight hours a day. No more! And it was enough, because my suggestions were indeed put in place very soon. We adopted one of three realistic scenarios, and I implemented it during the following months. The project that was abandoned before was reintroduced, together with a team of five for its implementation under my leadership. I didn't gloss over the facts of my burnout after my return, something my therapist had strongly advised against. It was such a relief not to have to play the role of the perfect super manager anymore. I sometimes allowed myself not to look for the ultimate solution and found it easier than before because the people around me were more considerate. To say *no* consistently was something I only had to learn years later. My colleagues' reactions varied from "You are much nicer now" to "You've lost your bite." But I definitely felt more at ease with myself. Inside, I wasn't overly involved anymore and could question myself and my work better.

My workload was not so demanding anymore, but inside, some things hadn't changed. More and more often, I questioned what I was doing. Why was I spending time over calculations and projections day after day? I enjoyed the leadership and the team workshops, but most of the time I sat in front of a computer, deeply engrossed in numbers and data. I nearly lost my mind if ever the figures didn't add up because of a mistake in the system. I envied my colleagues who loved data analysis and got excited when they could search for a mistake in the system. I could never generate any enthusiasm for abstract calculations, even though I tried time and again to learn more about tables, statistics, and data. It remained stressful and unsatisfying work for me.

As a balance to my work life, I had started to play solo gigs in a traditional old pub in Cologne. I invited friends and colleagues to my birthday party so I could act out my dream of being a pianist in a bar at least once. I sang and played a mixture of classics alongside my own compositions, and for an extra kick played the drums and cymbals with my feet!

My birthday concert was a great success, and the owner of the pub asked me whether I would like to do it on a regular basis. Ha, yes; I would like that! So, I performed there for more than two years, later also playing the guitar. In the end, I was even able to charge an entrance fee for my gigs. It boosted my confidence, which had dropped very low during the most recent crisis.

My relationship in Cologne didn't survive the phase of unemployment and lack of direction. I had been drawn too deeply into the maelstrom of defeat and self-doubt. Instead, I now embarked on a long-distance relationship with a woman I met at my brother's wedding. She lived in Göttingen. We discussed whether we might live together one day, but she couldn't move away from Göttingen because of her job and I didn't want to leave Cologne. In the summer of 2007, my friend Marco told me he was moving to Mallorca to live on a *finca*—a country estate. "Why don't you come too, and we can start up a musical project as a duo?" he said. "I'll sing and play the guitar; you sing and play the piano and percussion."

Hmm, why not have a sabbatical? I could switch off, recharge, and decide in peace and quiet whether or not to move to Göttingen. My gut said yes. Soon after, I went to see my boss and told him that at the end of the year I would resign and take some time out—to play music on Mallorca. Until then, I would meet all the important deadlines and hand everything over in a well-organized manner to my successor. It was like in Luxembourg. I had to get away without knowing exactly where I was going. But I had made my decision. I wanted to recalibrate and not allow inertia to keep me in a job that didn't satisfy me, even if it was going well. I stayed until the end of 2007 and handed over the now smooth-running project, as well as an efficient team, to my successor.

The year of 2008 was my year of leisure. Most of the time, Marco and I lived close to a small mountain village on Mallorca in an old finca in the middle of a sweet-smelling lemon and orange grove. The only other sound around was the bleating of sheep grazing everywhere. But it got noisy when we took our instruments to the nearby barn to rehearse for our gigs. We were probably the smallest unplugged rock 'n' roll band in the world. After a few weeks, we played in beach bars and at private parties. Named "Los Dos," meaning "The Two," we once managed to get onto the big stage in the bullfighting arena of Palma de Mallorca. I took regular intensive lessons in Spanish and improved my fluency on trips with Mallorquin friends. But most of all, I spent the time figuring out whether or not I would return to Göttingen.

Inspiration

A burnout is only the last point in a crisis that snuck up on you. Job burnout doesn't happen overnight; it's a response to continuous stress and excessive demands at work.

According to the World Health Organization (WHO), the three characteristics of "burn-out syndrome" are:

- Feelings of energy depletion or exhaustion
- Increased mental distance from one's job, or feelings of negativism or cynicism related to one's job
- Reduced professional efficacy

The definition is included in the 11th Revision of the International Classification of Diseases (ICD-11), a classification system for medical diagnoses adopted worldwide. So far, burn-out syndrome has only played a minor role in medical classification, even though it's known to be a widespread phenomenon. It's not seen as a disease itself, but as a "factor" that has an impact on health. It's a risk factor for depression.

You can prevent burnout by choosing one of the three options for dealing with a stressful situation: *leave it, love it,* or *change it.*

If the stressful situation doesn't resolve itself, sooner or later you will be forced to make a decision. The longer you postpone your decision and the consequent implementation of it, the more likely your body will take over and make the decision for you by burning out. It will say, "Leave it!" We should be grateful to our body for a reaction that liberates us, at least for a time, from a miserable situation. As such, burnout isn't the real problem, but a contribution to its solution.

Social support is an important protective factor in preventing burnout. It's important to get help when work gets too demanding instead of trying to do everything and isolating yourself. Be mindful of where you seek help. Real friends listen to you supportively and give you honest and constructive feedback. They encourage you to make changes in yourself and your situation and to leave the role of the victim behind. Friends who help friends in need aren't always pleasant, but they are the ones who take the friendship seriously. They talk to you in an open and honest way, not just comforting or pitying to please you. Real friends help you to help yourself. Of course, it's valuable when a friend helps you out by doing some jobs for you so you can manage your tight schedule at work. But if that leads to you burying yourself even deeper into your workload instead of tackling the root of the problem, such help can be counterproductive in the long run. Real friends have the courage to point this out to you and won't simply bow to your demands. They won't just give us what we want, but instead what we need—for example, uncomfortable and honest feedback. Advice from real friends can sometimes be so uncomfortable that we won't consider them our friends at all. The story of the cow and the mouse illustrates the point:

A mouse is running away from a cat, fighting for its life. It runs into a cowshed but can't find a suitable hiding place, so it hides in the shadow of a cow. The cow thinks, "I'll help that mouse" and drops a big cowpat on the little rodent to hide it. The cat sees the mouse's tail sticking out from the dung, pulls it out and eats it. And the moral of the story is:

1. *Not everyone shitting on you is an enemy.*
2. *Not everyone who pulls you out of shit is a friend.*

Consciously, see to it that you have a good social network that you can rely on in an emergency. It's better to have a few real friends than many superficial acquaintances who are out to please you. When in doubt, go and see an expert for honest advice and effective support.

Here are eleven suggestions that may help prevent burnout:

1. Choose a job that you like and is fun for you.
2. In an acutely stressful situation, ask your boss to decide on the top priorities. A good boss will thank you because he or she will be able to retain your services as a worker.
3. Sometimes say *no* to others when you feel it's too much. Say *yes* to yourself and your own needs more often.
4. Plan less, and often you will achieve more.
5. Take regular breaks. A little run or walk around the block can help to clear your head and recharge your batteries.
6. Eat healthily and drink enough water.
7. Take regular exercise without trying to achieve personal records.
8. Get enough sleep. Here's a tip for sleep problems in stressful times: guided sleep hypnosis can help you to drop off and sleep through.
9. Have regular time offline—no emails, texts, or messages.
10. Practice relaxation techniques such as meditation, yoga, or biofeedback.
11. Do without cigarettes and alcohol, and reduce your coffee consumption.

Tumbler Toy

There's a children's toy sometimes called a "roly-poly," or a "tumbler." It is like a symbol for resilience. You push it over and it gets up again. Children love it, because you can push it over time and time again, and it always returns to an upright position. But what is quite fun in a toy can have serious consequences in real life. If people behave like tumbler toys—they fall, they get up again, and carry on—then they will always tumble again at the same point, even if they managed to get up before. Why? Because people remain the same. They don't change easily, neither themselves, nor their position in life. It's as if they were made of wood, like a toy.

Why is it that some people make the same mistake time and time again without learning from it or changing something fundamental in their life? In my view, it's because they like to escape to a comfort zone after a crisis to recover from the painful experience.

But the longer they stay in their comfort zone, the less they feel the need to learn from the crisis and change something fundamental about their life. Often you hear sentences like, "Everything is alright again. It wasn't that bad, really. I'll just try again." That was definitely the case with me. On our sunny and tranquil finca in Spain, I quickly left behind my hectic city life. The memories of my unpleasant and unsatisfying office job—with the awful number-crunching and the pressure of deadlines—gradually faded into the background. Instead of processing it, I began to glorify it a bit. After all, I had gotten things together again after my burnout and had left my job on a peak of success. I had earned so much money that I could afford a year of downtime. It had only been a job, after all. Maybe in the next one I would have more fun.

My thoughts were more focused on my relationship and whether I should move to Göttingen. My girlfriend visited me on Mallorca, and we had a lovely time together. When she left again, I missed her very much. That tipped the balance. I decided to move to Göttingen. Now all I had to do was look for a job in the area.

Back to Göttingen

I began to write applications for jobs. After a short while, I was offered a contract to work as regional manager for a management consultancy in Hanover. Great, I thought. I can enjoy city life again, something I had always liked since my student days.

Shortly before I signed the contract, I got invited to an interview with a medical technology company near Göttingen for the position of senior controller. That was about the last thing I wanted to do, and on top of it in a small town! But I didn't want to miss out on the chance for a paid flight home, as I had planned to go back to Göttingen anyway to look for a flat for my girlfriend and me.

In the interview, I learned that the job wasn't a controller position as such, but would be more strategic. It would be dealing with facts and figures, but also involved international travel and was more of a consultancy position. That intrigued me. Then came the decisive question. "What would you like to be the icing on the cake if you worked for us?" I answered that I would like to improve my Spanish so I could better undertake projects in South America. To my amazement, they immediately replied, "Okay. Let's do it." Shortly afterwards, I signed a contract with Ottobock HealthCare GmbH, a world leader in technical orthopedics.

I started in January 2008, and was immediately at full speed. The complexity and the number and variety of the projects was breathtaking. My boss was a highly intelligent and analytical person, and I could learn a lot from him. In time, we developed a relationship built on trust and mutual respect. I had been lucky; again, I had a boss who believed in me 100 percent. It felt so good! He actually had more confidence in me than I had, and soon I was handed responsibility for demanding projects, such as the coordination of strategic development of markets in Brazil and Argentina. I flew to South America a few times and held workshops in Spanish with our local subsidiaries and key customers.

I was giddy with success and threw myself into numerous projects, always attempting to achieve more. The amount of recognition grew proportionally to the number of overtime hours I put in. My relationship with my girlfriend began to suffer. In the beginning, it was hardly noticeable as my girlfriend, who worked freelance, was also a workaholic. But at some point, we concluded that splitting up would be best for both of us. Again, another relationship had gone down the drain. The separation made me very sad, and with every piece of furniture I carried from our shared flat, I felt that I was burying one of my dreams. The vision of eternal love and a family again seemed far away. And I was already in my late thirties …

But I'm a tumbler toy, I thought, I'll just get up again, dust myself off, and carry on. After all, I now had more time for my job without feeling guilty. I also enjoyed the best parts of being a single again. It didn't take long before I was attracted to another woman. Over time, the affair developed into a relationship. I enjoyed being validated as a man and liked the magic of a new relationship.

At work, there was a discussion as to whether I would consider leading a department in a growing team higher up the ladder. I would have said *yes* to the leadership aspect, because I liked the contact with people and the coordination of group processes. But again, I felt a bit reluctant about taking on high-flying projects based on numbers.

So, I didn't pursue it further, as the position had not been officially advertised anyway. The resolution came automatically a short time later. But before that I had to learn again the hard way that abstract number-crunching was really not my thing.

One Last Battle with the Numbers

Together with a team of other controllers, I was responsible for the coordination of the company's mid-term planning. We had to make projections for turnover and costs for thousands of products in more than fifty countries for the next five years. A veritable blizzard of data sheets had to be analyzed, evaluated, and amalgamated. For months on end, I was drowning in numbers, looking for mistakes, doing the odd night shift—and slowly burning out again. Again, I was lying awake at night wondering what I was actually fighting so hard for. I felt detached from the benefits my work was creating. I knew that our planning would secure the financial future of the company. I was conscious that our customers would benefit, and people with missing limbs would get high-quality prostheses in the end. Rationally, it was all okay. But emotionally, I wasn't involved. I was too far removed from our customers, so for me, my work again was about abstract analyses of numbers without any concrete connection to real life. I was desperate and knew that I couldn't go on like this. But what could I do? At rock bottom, I was finally saved.

Inspiration

If you behave like a tumbler toy, don't be amazed when you fall down in the same place again and again. "Fall down, get up. Dust yourself off, carry on"—this cycle creates a merry-go-round of crises. To get off it, you first of all need to reflect on it. Once you have got up again, perhaps you should look for a new direction.

The Turning Point

The Owl Episode

It was a cold January evening, and after twelve or thirteen hours of high-octane work, I was driving a colleague home. We were on a country road and it was dark. We used the time to discuss a project because the deadline for presenting the report on it was imminent. How could we analyze the numbers better? Should we add another column to the Excel sheet and calculate an interim result? But maybe we could ... Then there was a bump, a dull thump on my side of the car, which interrupted our discussion. My foot hit the brake, I got out, and walked back a few meters. In the moonlight, I saw an owl sitting by the side of the road. It was just sitting there.

As it happens, only a short while before, my girlfriend's father—an enthusiastic birdwatcher—and I had visited an owl expert in the area. The man ran an owl sanctuary near Göttingen where he looked after injured and sick birds. He showed us the cages and described with great enthusiasm what had happened to his patients. Most of the owls had broken a wing after a collision with a car. But the problem, he explained, was that they would try to fly off with the broken wing as soon as the shock subsided. But if the wing couldn't be saved, they would have to spend the rest of their lives in an aviary. And that's if they were brought to him at all. The thing to do was to grab the injured owl from behind with a blanket as long as it was in shock and bring it directly to him. He had advised us urgently, "Please always carry a blanket in the car, just in case!"

I had followed his advice and put a blanket in my car's trunk. Now I was holding it and carefully approached the owl from behind, but I completely underestimated how strong the bird was. In order not to squeeze it too much, I only put the blanket loosely around it, and with a few beats of its wings it got free and flew off. But its flight was smooth and elegant, so its wings must have survived intact: My colleague confirmed the assumption when she realized how unhappy I was about the failed rescue attempt. The owl seemed to be okay!

This night-time event somehow struck me as magical and became a kind of key experience. When the owl hit my car, the abstract world of numbers faded into the background. It was like an alarm call from life itself; the owl reminded me that there was a real world out there. I felt clarity as I did in the night of my kidnapping on the boat. Back then, I knew exactly what I was fighting for—my survival and that of my parents. That gave me strength and the feeling of doing something meaningful. And now I had the same feeling again. I knew exactly why I was doing what I was doing: walking in the night in my posh suit to rescue an owl instead of driving on. I could do something tangible to turn a life around. In this case, it was the life of an owl.

I felt full of energy and fulfilled like I hadn't for a long time. I swore, I want more of this feeling, especially at work. For the first time in my life, I searched seriously for my inner calling, a clear purpose. I stopped being a tumbler toy. That was about ten years after my kidnapping.

The Kick in the Butt

Shortly after the episode with the owl, I had another significant experience. This time it was something very mundane, but it felt like a kick in the butt. On the whole, in my experience, there are two kinds of watershed moments or triggers. Sometimes one experiences a magical moment, when things click into place and one is offered the chance to change one's life for the better. At other times, one suffers a crisis that forces a change one would never dare to make voluntarily.

My relationship with my girlfriend was exciting; I loved her sense of humor and that she was able to laugh at herself. And she was so refreshingly spontaneous. On a whim, we might take an inflatable dinghy and some paddles down the river for a bit. Or we might go for a hike without a particular destination and stop for a meal somewhere. It was all wonderfully unplanned and the polar opposite to my working day where every minute was tightly scheduled.

We were a good couple, but I remained non-committal regarding our future. I had it in the back of my mind that I wanted to have a family soon, but as she would be graduating shortly, she was keen to prioritize getting a foot on the career ladder. The longer we were together, the more the question of whether we had a future together edged into the foreground. But still, I wouldn't commit myself. Understandably, she wasn't happy with that and decided to move to Frankfurt after her graduation to make a new start.

On the day that would change my life, we had an argument. I don't remember anymore what triggered it, probably my lack of commitment to anything. But I remember well how it went and how the day ended. We blamed and accused each other for hours. I felt I was in the right and tried to remain calm and rational, but that seemed to make her even more angry. At some point things escalated, and her accusations turned to blows aimed below the belt. I then started to shout as well. What was she on about? Her answer echoed in my mind. In a nutshell, she shouted: "Stop putting the blame on me all the time. Have a look at yourself. You have a fucking problem. You have no idea what you want. That's why you can't even have an argument. You avoid every conflict and every decision."

It wasn't the first time I had heard this in a relationship. But at that moment, for the first time, I thought it possible that there was a deeper truth in the accusations. It was like a revelation: there's a pattern in my life that keeps repeating. It can't be a coincidence. It must have something to do with me! The problem is *me* and not the women.

Before I could recover, my girlfriend slammed the door shut behind her in fury. There I was. Alone, left with the most painful insight of my life. I wasn't the hero I had thought. Quite the opposite. Suddenly, I saw very clearly that I had a giant blind spot, a pattern repeated through many relationships. Maybe I had been lying to myself all my life. I was dizzy with shame and fear, but one thing was clear: if I continued like this I would always end up in the same place and never have a long-term, happy relationship. If I didn't want to forget my dream of having a family, I needed to change something, and that was me. At least if I acknowledged the problem was with me, I could find the solution to it. I was convinced and started a search for reasons and solutions.

Today, I'm very grateful for that kick in the butt. This crisis had been absolutely necessary. In my misery, I was forced to change and turn my life around for the better. Some people need more than one crisis, as well as great pain, before they are ready to change. It helped that, after the episode with the owl, I had already opened up a bit to the possibility of change. I had started to look ahead. And this kick in the butt propelled me further.

In hindsight, I realized what steps are necessary not only to get through a crisis but also to grow from it personally. It's not easy. And not very pleasant. But it's possible, step by little step.

Inspiration

The watershed moments in life often follow a crisis, which force people to make changes. But sometimes there is also a hint from fate pointing you in the right direction and you will find an opportunity to turn your life toward something better. But it's necessary to notice when that opportunity comes, to recognize it and to acknowledge it. When you use this opportunity to change, you can avoid repeating the same mistakes and crises over and over again.

Growing from a Crisis — Step by Step

Everyone copes with a crisis in their own way. But the process can be split into typical phases that most people go through. According to the Swedish psychiatry professor Johan Cullberg, there are four phases:

1. *Shock phase:* Initially we distance ourselves from the challenging event and don't want to know about it. This phase, when we split the pain off, is shaped by a feeling of emptiness.
2. *Reaction phase:* We begin to confront the painful facts, but without owning them. It causes a roller-coaster of emotions: fear, pain, anger, and rage, but also joy.
3. *Processing phase:* We take responsibility again for our life by accepting our painful loss. We look for ways and means to deal with the changed reality with hope.
4. *New direction phase:* We let go of the pain and open up to the world around us again. The loss is replaced by new people or objects. The event can lead to new insights, values, and patterns of behavior.

This four-phase model doesn't necessarily have to be followed step by step. One can alternate between the phases or repeat them. But it's crucial to skip neither the second painful phase nor to get stuck in it. Coping with a crisis is an exhaustive process, but at the end of it is the chance for personal growth.

"That which does not kill us makes us stronger," Nietzsche wrote in his 1889 work *Twilight of the Idols.* Modern research seems to confirm this, as the renowned neuroscientist Raffael Kalisch concludes in his book about resilience, *Der Resiliente Mensch: Wie Wir Krisen Erleben und Bewältigen* (*The Resilient Person: How We Experience and Cope with Crises*). He calls it post-traumatic growth when survivors of serious accidents talk of the positive influence it had on their lives. I felt it too after my release. Through the experience of captivity and guerrilla warfare, I learned to really appreciate freedom and peace, and to this day consider both a very precious gift.

But one effect that I had clearly anticipated didn't occur. I had assumed that after my extreme experience in the jungle, nothing would ever seriously stress me again. My burnout taught me the opposite. I've asked myself how this could have happened and came to an interesting explanation.

For years, I had the wrong images in my head of what coping in a crisis meant. And I'm convinced that visualizations have an effect on you. The roly-poly toy was one of the images. It was my role model for successfully coping with a crisis. But it caused me to end up on a never-ending carousel of crises. Now I can see that this is inevitable if you refuse to grow from the experience each time you fall down. Maybe the expression "grow-up toy" would be more appropriate, because instead of a static figure you would imagine an organic growth process.

For years, I had assumed that crises were not very valuable. For me, critical events were just hurdles that had to be cleared to keep on running. That had been a mantra. Today, I don't consider a crisis a hurdle but rather see it as a step. Thus, life turns into a staircase. Every crisis means I can reach a higher step, as long as I make use of the opportunity to grow. Climbing stairs is still quite arduous, but at least the process makes sense. The stairs take me up, toward a higher plane of development. I don't consider a crisis as a friend necessarily, but it is at least an ally that helps me to get out of a comfort zone and offers a chance for personal growth. This attitude helps me to deal with life in a more relaxed way.

Stages

Serenely let us move to distant places
And let no sentiments of home detain us.
The Cosmic Spirit seeks not to restrain us
But lifts us stage by stage to wider spaces.
If we accept a home of our own making,
Familiar habit makes for indolence.
We must prepare for parting and leave-taking
Or else remain the slave of permanence.

Hermann Hesse

This excerpt from Hermann Hesse's poem "Stages" is about letting go and it is about departure. The poem also contains the phrase "in all beginnings dwells a magic force." And this, even in the hour of death. The comforting words paint a picture of life as a journey that lets us grow, step by step. It reminds me of the computer games I loved playing as a child. As the hero, I had to fight monsters in labyrinths to get to the next level. The monsters became bigger and bigger, level by level, until I was confronted with the final opponent. When I had beaten him, I won the game. "The whole life is a game," the author Hape Kerkeling says. In that sense, death is the final opponent. This reflects Buddhist philosophy: for your whole life you practice letting go and prepare yourself for death.

But now we leave theories, poetry, games, and religion behind and go back to 'practical' things. What steps help us to cope with a crisis and make us stronger? The following three steps enable you to get off the carousel of crises and turn your life around:

1. *Accept the crisis:* Mourn your losses instead of denying them or glossing over them. Accept the need to act—it can't go on like this.
2. *Look for opportunities/chances:* Learn from the experience, recognize the need to change, and the opportunity for personal growth.
3. *Dare to make changes:* Don't go back to old patterns,

but utilize the power of the crisis to courageously seek out new directions.

Those three steps correspond to phases two through four of Cullberg's "Phase Model." The focus is less on merely coping in a crisis and more on personal growth. Using the example of my own experience, in the following pages I'll focus on the stumbling blocks and pitfalls of a crisis leading to a new and better future.

First Step: Accept the Crisis

I had to recognize and acknowledge first that I was in a crisis and also to accept that things couldn't go on as before. Previously, after a relationship breakup, I would simply have dusted myself off and moved on. To save myself from any blame, I would have told myself that it had nothing to do with me, but that I was in a relationship with the wrong woman. I would have had no difficulties explaining away the breakup as owing to my girlfriend's peculiarities. I would have washed my hands of any responsibility. I was sure to have the support of my friends and family who were always on my side and would have carried on as before. I would be looking for recognition from women what a damn fantastic guy I was. Eventually I would have glossed over the breakup with the words "It would never have worked out. Now I'm free again, and there are plenty of fish in the sea."

But this time I was no tumbler toy anymore—thank God. I didn't get up and carry on as before. I stopped, stayed on the ground, and tried to grasp my pitiful situation. I mourned the relationship, which probably had much more potential and depth than I had thought. I confessed to myself that my part in its failure was probably bigger than I wanted to acknowledge. I knew that I had quite a few skeletons in the relationship cupboard, the victims of my pattern of behavior. My girlfriend had pushed open the door to this cupboard by holding a mirror in front of my face. "Have a look at yourself, you seem to have a fucking problem." There was no way out. I was forced to have a good look into the cupboard and tidy up.

There was no way out. I was forced to go down into the basement of my mind to tidy up thoroughly. It was hard, this insight, but strangely comforting as well. I had fallen down and was on the ground, but I didn't feel down. It was more of a sense that, having reached rock bottom, from now on things could only get better. It's easier to push yourself up again when you are at the bottom, rather than to try swimming against a current.

Full of courage and confidence, I started my search for the opportunity that might come about from this painful experience. At work, too, I had the feeling that I had reached a watershed. It couldn't go on as before. Previously,

I had always glossed over things with lines like, "It's a very stressful project, but it'll be over some time soon." If you find yourself saying "Close your eyes and get through it" when you're in a crisis, don't be surprised when you overlook opportunities for change. Now I had opened my eyes and discovered an uncomfortable truth that would hopefully save me: I'm in the wrong job. And the responsibility for that was all mine. I had chosen it, after all, or at least accepted the offer when it was made. How could I complain about it? I'm not a hostage to my boss, but a free person who can make decisions about his future. But that exactly was my problem. I simply didn't know what kind of work I wanted to do. And now I wanted to find out the reasons behind it.

I told my boss about the magical encounter with the owl and what effect it had had on me. From now on I wanted more "owl experiences" in my life. I could talk to him openly, because our relationship was good. He liked me, and so at first, he only smiled at me, slightly puzzled, and then asked: "What do you mean, owl experiences?"

I couldn't give him a clear answer—I hadn't come that far. "How about coaching, to help people to develop," I said. "But nothing abstract and involving numbers." We had a good talk. It was very liberating because I had taken a first step toward a change. I could think more clearly again. In a follow-up conversation I suggested, "I'll finish the current projects and then concentrate on ones with less number-crunching and more human involvement. And I'll reduce my working hours to train as a counselor and to do some research about burnout."

He agreed. I was very grateful for our open and honest talk.

Second Step:
Looking for Opportunities

Before, after a private or professional crisis, I simply walked on and missed the chance to grow from it. I just tried it all over again—a new game, looking for new luck. But this time it was different. Instead of seeking my fortune somewhere out there, I started the search inside myself. I considered:

- What can I learn from my crises?
- What do they have to do with me?
- How can I change so my life gets better?

I started to sniff for truths like a pig hunting truffles. I had nothing to lose, I thought, even if I found out that I was the problem. But that would be good, because then I could resolve the problem myself!

I won't be a victim of circumstances anymore—no pawn of fate—and I won't end up as a tragic antihero. I will know what is going on and can take my fate into my own hands. I guessed it would be a long and arduous journey, and I was right about that. But I had already taken the first step, which definitely was the most difficult.

The first station on my journey to the destination named "personal development" was my training as a counselor specializing in burnout. At the same time, I took some excursions in other directions. Within three years, I spent more than one hundred days in personality coaching, taking journeys through the Swedish wilderness, attending seminars on self-knowledge, and undertaking traditional initiations and weeks of silence in a retreat, among other things. I was stretched to my limits time and again. It felt as if I was dying a thousand deaths, saying goodbye to some of the lies I had told myself all my life. I had always thought myself a considerate person whose priority was to meet other people's requests. I thought I was someone who didn't have to argue because I was above such things. But, at best, that was only part of my truth. I had an uncomfortable insight when I realized that I didn't have a vision of my life for which I was prepared to seriously fight. I was addicted to harmony and avoided conflicts like the plague. I looked for praise and recognition at all costs.

In relationships of the heart, I wasn't a man who knew what he wanted, rather I was a people pleaser who continuously tried to meet every wish and demand of others. I offered understanding and easy playfulness in the hope I would get love and recognition in return. That went well for a while, but once the honeymoon was over, the first conflicts arose. I avoided them and tried to placate others, as I had never learned to argue in my sheltered childhood. Now I know that's not a good foundation for a long-term, healthy relationship.

At work, I always simply did what my bosses demanded of me. It remained a simple transaction—achievement for recognition. In order not to disappoint my boss, I exceeded even the most unreasonable demands. Even when my body was in the red zone already, my foot was still on the pedal. I could never say *no* because it would have meant rejection and conflict.

I realized that never in my life had I actually taken the lead. I'd simply carried out other people's decisions instead of making them myself. In Luxembourg, before the kidnapping, I even handed over my future to the universe and had asked for a hint from fate. In that sense, I was in my element during my captivity. I didn't have to make any decisions anymore but had to 'just' survive.

This process of self-exploration was very painful but also beneficial and healing. I didn't only find out who I was, but most of all, what I wanted. A clearer vision of my life was slowly developing. I wanted a dynamic relationship with a strong, independent, and attractive woman with whom I could have a family and grow old. In my vision, she dreamed of children like I did, and found just as much fulfilment in her role as a mother as I would as a father. Together we would live an international life and love it. Professionally, we would follow our hearts. My personal mission I had found already—I wanted to support other people and help them be happy, successful, and healthy.

Thanks to this inner clarity, I finally managed to take responsibility for my life. In addition, I was ready and willing to take on external responsibility, perhaps as a father. But for the first time, I was also motivated to take the next step professionally, on my own initiative. In a leadership role, I wanted to work with people, for people. Previously, I always had to be coaxed by my boss into taking responsibility for staff. As a person keen on maintaining harmony, this meant things I was always afraid of: taking on leadership roles, developing visions, bearing responsibility, making decisions, pushing through targets, resolving conflicts, accepting rejection. I was full of respect for executives who would stick their head above the parapet and become an easy target. Previously, I had always been able to defer to my boss who had asked me to do this or that.

But now, I wanted to take on leadership roles, to work with people and for people so the world would become a better place.

To prepare me to take on a leadership role, my boss sent me on an intensive coaching program for executives. Jürgen Dluzniewski, a wonderful coach, worked with me on the so-called "Essence Model." It was very worthwhile. At the end of it, I was able to express in one sentence what life tasks I was envisioning and why I was suitable for this. "I am the person who values people and gives them honest feedback so that they can be open and trusting and grow personally." Now I had the inner clarity to take on responsibility in a leadership role—and I also wanted it!

Third Step: Dare to Change

Man is a creature of habit. Most people find change difficult. Even when things get unpleasant, they still stick to their old habits and say, "Better the devil you know." I know that too well because I have been a real fan of comfort zones since my childhood. My life has been quite varied so far and I consider myself adaptable to change, but I could never take the important steps necessary for growth in work and in love. I simply lacked the courage to tackle them.

That my life today is happy and successful is not due to me always knowing what I wanted and pursuing my goals with courage. In fact, I owe it to the crises I suffered. They made me the person I am today. I have learned to know and appreciate them as valuable "aid workers."

A crisis is painful and always will be. But a crisis is often an opportunity that has to be grasped, a gateway to the future. But that doesn't work if you always just get up from a fall and carry on walking. After getting up, you have to stop and learn from the experience, to change, and possibly find a new direction.

For me, my crises always were valuable signposts for what I needed to change in my life to make it better. The kidnapping was a hint from fate that showed me how strong I could be when I fought for something that felt important to me. My burnout was the clear indication that I was in the wrong job and had to learn to set better boundaries. The breakups in my private life gave me the feedback to point out the blind spots in my personality.

But I had averted my eyes for too long and missed chances. Only when I was in my late thirties, when the pain and desperation were overwhelming, did I start to look at and use the crises as something else: aid workers.

Once you stop reducing a crisis to its component parts of pain and destruction and focus instead on the hidden opportunities, you can turn them into friends and allies for life. Crises are a part of life. The question is not *whether* there will be another crisis, but *when* it will be. As we must suffer them anyway, we should at least use the chances they offer to grow through them. We need to look in the right direction: forward. It's always good when we can endow our painful experiences with a sense of the future.

I have had the good fortune to meet a lot of people in my life who have made the best of their fate. There was a woman who survived life-threatening cancer and today says that only afterwards did she learn to appreciate her health as a gift. There was a man from a difficult background, who slid into criminality and prison, but who today offers courses in the prevention of violence. Or the man who lost his lower leg when he was nine because of cancer and today says, "If I could get my leg back in exchange for my life today, I wouldn't want it." His name is Heinrich Popow, one of the most successful sprinters in the world. He works with young talents and motivates people who have had a limb amputated.

It's a paradox that very often positive things develop from negative events. It's a good idea to prepare your mind for the chances that might be hidden behind life's unavoidable setbacks.

In that sense, I'd like to give you eight suggestions that will help sharpen your instincts for how you too can grow in a crisis—something you probably have done already without noticing it:

1. *Appreciate life*: Accept and understand the finality of life—every day could be your last. Live consciously in the here and now. Enjoy the good moments that you might have taken for granted before—a sunset, for example.
2. *Develop more serenity*: Don't get upset about trivial things. Develop the confidence to cope with difficult situations that may arise in the future. Trust in your inner strength.
3. *Discover new opportunities*: Many restrictions in your life reveal unexpected opportunities to do something that you wouldn't or couldn't do without

this restriction. Wheelchair sports is one such example. There can be new ways of living, occupations, or hobbies.

4. *Live more healthily*: A negative experience can be an alarm signal to do a better job looking after your health. The consequences of your choices might lead you to stop smoking or to never use your phone again while driving.
5. *Get involved*: Help other people who are in a similar position as you. Pass on your own lessons from it, maybe in a self-help group. People who have lost a loved one are particularly valuable when working with bereavement, for example.
6. *Personal growth*: Hard blows in life often are the impetus to grapple with one's self. People explore their inner being to find out what to do, what is really important in life.
7. *Faith and spirituality*: Many people begin to pray in a life crisis and find a path to faith that will give them strength on their further journey. An increased interest in existential questions, such as the meaning of life, can be pursued independently from a religion and give strength.
8. *Finding friends for life*: Often, we meet real friends when we are at rock bottom. They will support us in difficult times, give us strength, and honest feedback. It's a good idea to deepen those friendships and let relationships go that are less nurturing.

Consider these suggestions as ideas for your own process of self-reflection. It feels good when you manage to gain something positive from a negative event. At the same time it's okay if it doesn't happen, and you carry on suffering from a traumatic experience. It would be counterproductive if the positive suggestions put additional pressure on you or trigger feelings of guilt. Don't think, "It's all my fault if I can't find anything positive in my experience." For that reason, I'll warn you of the tyranny of the popular school of positive thinking and "self-optimizing." I'll repeat: the suggestions in this book are meant to be "inspirations" rather than decrees. You will realize yourself what is helpful for you and what is not. My attitude here is, "I'm okay as I am; you're okay as you are."

I can say today that I live a fulfilling life, and not despite my crises, but because of them. They were all necessary. They have vigorously pushed me out of my comfort zone and forced me to grow. Many of the fateful blows that I suffered have really been nudges or thrusts in the right direction.

Fate has dealt me a good hand. It shook me awake with an owl and then gave me a kick in the butt. And when I was finally ready to aspire to leadership, I was given the opportunity for it. After my coaching, I was ready to take my chances, that is, to recognize and to grasp them.

As it happened, I heard that Ottobock was planning to advertise for a top executive. "I want to do it!" I said immediately. The person I was with at the time gave me a puzzled look and asked, "Are you sure? You want to climb up the ladder that high?" But I was absolutely sure. A short while ago I had been the project manager responsible for one of seven departments in this area, an international school for orthopedic technicians. I had gotten to know a completely new world and learned to love it. Orthopedic technicians and therapists are dedicated to their mission, and I found this very touching. They are keen to make people who have lost a limb because of an accident or other misfortune mobile again. They also construct specially designed wheelchairs and orthotics for people who still have all their limbs but have lost the neural contact to move them. When patients learn to walk again, thanks to their sophisticated prostheses, most of them cry. And the therapists and technicians involved are equally moved by it. I always missed those touching moments in my previous jobs, but now there was an opportunity to do exactly what I had wanted so much: to work with people for people.

In October 2013, I faced my new team of sixty and introduced myself as a leader who "appreciates people and gives them honest feedback so they can trust him to be open and develop." My inner clarity gave me the courage to take this on, a task for which I never before would have had the confidence. I now felt I could follow a thread to guide me in the right direction. It didn't only guide me, but also my team. Appreciation and clear and open feedback were the central elements for me to reach my targets as an executive, while at the same time supporting people in their personal growth. I was also able to carry out uncomfortable tasks as an executive, such as moving staff to different positions or dismissing them. I was able to stay true to my inner values while being transparent with my team.

What followed were five successful years that I enjoyed very much. I'm not saying that there was no stress. Quite the opposite. The challenges of leading such a large team of experienced executives was enormous, but it was fulfilling because the ability to grow in this area meant so much to me. It was primarily about people and not about numbers. Every day I could watch as people in a wheelchair who had lost limbs came and to us from all over the world and, a short time later, went back to their lives walking upright. I could directly help my colleagues fulfill their jobs with the passion and success they wanted. Even when I had to fight for our budget and had to juggle numbers, I always knew for certain why I was doing it—for my colleagues and our clients.

In my private life, too, I rose from the ashes like a phoenix. Instead of throwing myself into the next available affair, I started looking for a woman with whom I wanted to start a family. I eventually met her at a seminar for personal growth, and it was quite intense, because she was anything but easy. She was not a woman looking for a man who had helper syndrome or who needed someone to flatter his ego. She was a wild horse, impulsive and full of *joie de vivre*. It didn't start off as a cozy romance, but as a wild ride through many highs and lows and honest encounters. We were serious, because if it was for the long run, we'd better make sure we checked each other carefully. This time I wasn't just after a short romance. I was in the starting blocks for a fulfilling life—as a couple, with children …

Spoiler alert! There is a happy ending—at least for the time being. These days, I am living the dream of a happily married family man in every respect. I love my wife from the bottom of my heart. After her career in an international management consultancy, she has found fulfilment as a mother and manager of the family and enjoys her freedom to also work as a yoga teacher and psychotherapist. We are very different. She is spontaneous; whereas I'm more the reliable planner. We complement each other very well. But conflicts in everyday life are, of course, factored in. I was expecting this when I took a courageous step out of my comfort zone of people-pleasing relationships. Our relationship is lively, and it grows; we give each other honest feedback and learn from each other all the time. She learns from me to stop and reflect sometimes; and I from her to argue my case. I have come to love our conflicts as cleansing thunderstorms.

Despite all our differences in everyday life, my wife and I share something fundamentally important: our life plan is identical. Our family is our top priority. We love to spend time with our children and to bring them up together. We love living in Göttingen, close to my parents and my brother. At the same time, we share the love of the wider world and the chance to discover ourselves on our travels. Between us, we have moved to a new house about thirty times, mostly across borders and language barriers. The most important thing, though, is that we speak a common language when difficult decisions are on the table.

Inspiration

A crisis is painful and will always be painful, so you better use the opportunity to grow from it. The following three steps will help:

1. *Accept a crisis*: Stop and think and mourn what was lost. Accept your pain, instead of glossing over the situation. Recognize that things can't go on like before. A crisis is a challenge and an invitation to accept changes.
2. *Seek opportunities*: What can I learn from the crisis? Am I part of the problem? (That would be good because then I can find the solution within me.) What can I change to turn my life around?
3. *Dare to change*: Don't go on as before and fall back into old patterns. Use the crisis as a powerful push

> by fate to stride out on a new path that you never dared to take before or have deferred out of laziness.

A long time ago, Heraclitus, the Greek philosopher, said that the only constant thing in life is change. Life is meant to be growth. Quite often, a crisis is the result of changes that were postponed but were necessary for growth. Instead of rejecting growth, we should integrate it proactively into our life plan. Therefore:

- Accept that changes are part of life.
- Create changes in your life proactively and constantly.
- Use a crisis as a chance to make changes and grow.

Let me explain those three principles to make it easier to accept them and integrate them into your life.

To accept and integrate change doesn't mean that we are not allowed to enjoy the beautiful parts of life. Sometimes it's good to party on the spur of the moment and to enjoy periods of relaxation. After difficult times, it's important to stop and recharge. But then life goes on because change is part of it. Keep moving, so things remain lively, whether in your relationship, your work, or your health. Don't stop, don't get too comfortable in your job, but look for new challenges offering further opportunities to grow. Relationships need to be nurtured too. They remain lively if you grow *with* each other and get stronger together, but if you grow *into* each other, you become rigid. *Keep moving* is the motto.

This, of course, applies to your health as well. It's not only about fighting illness but keeping fit at all times. We repeatedly have to overcome the sloth inside us who would love it much more to lie on the sofa watching television.

Life sometimes feels like you're trapped in a long series of roadworks. Do you know the feeling? You finally get past one section and then the next one appears right behind it. The smooth times seem to be the exception. We would love to magically cast away those awful stretches and glide smoothly through the rest of our life. But it doesn't happen—neither in life nor on the roads. But remember, we also get stressed by potholes, diversions, and narrow roads, and often say, "Someone has to do something about it!" That's how we end up with roadworks.

In the long run, roadworks are a good investment, because problem spots get resolved. But they are hated in the short term because they slow us down. Often, people stuck in a traffic jam in a section of road under repair get annoyed and even honk their horn. We feel like victims of circumstance, but we are actually part of the problem. It's not "I'm in a traffic jam," but "I *am* the traffic jam."

It's a question of perspective as to whether we consider road works a problem or a solution. After all, they are necessary to guarantee smooth traffic flow. Without them we would risk our lives on bad roads or be forced on long diversions until the increase in traffic would bring everything to a standstill anyway.

Life is like a network of roads. Before we start working on it, we try to muddle through. We say, "It'll be okay—somehow," or "It'll resolve itself," or "I've got too much on my mind to deal with that now," or "Mustn't make a fuss." Of course, we can always try to avoid tackling a problem for a while, but at some point, it'll catch up with us. For that reason, it's a good idea to deal with unpopular changes as soon as possible rather than risk a bigger crisis in the long run.

Many life crises are the result of postponed repair work. Here are four examples to illustrate the point:

Relationships: The first sign of something wrong is that you don't talk to each other anymore, and then at some point, you drift apart and split up. A possible repair would be an open conversation, personal growth, and couples' therapy.

Work: At first you feel stressed and constantly run into difficulties with colleagues. What follows is burnout. Possible repair work includes coaching, a conversation with your boss, a personality test, or a change of job.

Health: It starts with recurring back problems, then pain, so you change posture to relieve it, and take painkillers. But in the end, it's a disc prolapse. Possible repair work includes physiotherapy, keeping good posture, or swimming rather than marathon running.

Finances: You don't have enough money to cover your living costs, leading to more debts, more interest to pay, and, in the end, bankruptcy. Possible repair work includes taking stock, setting a budget, saving money by doing without things, and maybe consulting a debt advisor.

Everyone has phases in their life when things don't run smoothly. That's quite normal. It only gets critical when problems intensify and turn into a crisis. It's always a good idea to intervene early. The knack is to recognize signs of deterioration and take courageous steps before the situation escalates.

What is your life like? Do you know where your possible sites for repair work are? How do you deal with them? Ask yourself the following questions to recognize needs for action and possibilities for change.

- In what area of my life are there "potholes"? Do I have constant stress at work? Relationship trouble? Constant physical or mental pain? Recurring or escalating money problems?
- How do other people perceive my need for repair works? Do I have blind spots? Which of my friends could give me honest feedback?
- What has kept me from tackling the problems already? What am I afraid of? Have I tried anything to solve the problem? Why hasn't it worked so far? How could I deal with it differently?

– What kind of support could help me? Where would I find it? Do I have role models? Are there inspiring books that address my problems? Are there any professionals who could help me?

If you attempt to answer those questions honestly and make the necessary changes at an early stage, you are on your way to avert a growing crisis. It's encouraging to know that we don't have to surrender helplessly to a life crisis and are able to improve our situation a good deal. But sometimes fate deals you an unexpected blow. A serious accident, a life-threatening illness, or the loss of a loved one can turn your life upside down in a moment. Sometimes events like this occur all at once. Most people feel helpless at first in these situations. The horse has bolted. The stable door is wide open.

What can we do when a life crisis cannot be averted anymore? It makes sense to make the best of the situation. "Making the best of it" doesn't mean that everything will be alright, because in the long run, glossing over things is just as unproductive as moaning about them. It's important to properly acknowledge the seriousness and the pain of the situation without becoming a victim. When we actively tackle an issue, we can influence the present as well as the future. In this context, the wisdom of chess is quite comforting. "It doesn't matter how bad your situation is, there's always a good next move." We can never "win" in life, and at some point, we will be in checkmate and will die. But we don't stop living because of this certainty. Quite the opposite! We should aim to make the best of our current situation and concentrate on the most important people and issues in our life.

The Treasure Trove of Life Experiences

I would be very happy if, when you're reading this book, you gain ideas for positively dealing with the setbacks in your life. A crisis often is reduced to its devastating effect—and that shouldn't be denied. But it's also important to focus on the creative potential inherent in many life crises.

Crises and misfortunes are considered deeply shameful in many cultures, and for that reason, they are very often kept secret. All the sharp corners and edges in one's life get sanded down or photoshopped. However, I can't claim that my honesty was always rewarded. My application for a consultancy position was rejected because I had been open about my kidnapping experience. I thought that it would be regarded positively or at least tolerated, but it was considered a problem.

When a negative life experience isn't acknowledged by one's social circle or at work, I think that it's not only hurtful and disrespectful but also an awful waste of human potential. All that experience remains unused. It's even worse when people deny their past crises to themselves, forget them, or repress them. Put the lid on, gloss over. After a traumatic event, this might be a protective response that makes psychological sense. But in most cases, we deny ourselves valuable lessons if we simply draw a line through our past. Many people do this, though, as I've done for years. We are too fearful to take a closer look and to process the event in an honest way. In the end, one might discover an unpleasant truth, as I did, when it dawned on me that I had played a large part in the failure of my relationships and jobs.

An honest look at our past can be frightening, but wouldn't it be nice if we could learn enough from our experiences to be able to look the future in the eye with confidence and strength? After all, fate could deal us another blow any minute and set us spinning again on the crisis carousel. Most people worry about their future when they are feeling okay. As a happy family man and successful executive, I was worried at times that everything would come crashing down at some point. The worry was well-founded, as I later found out.

We cannot always prevent a crisis, but we can steel ourselves against one. The necessary armor is often found in our own treasure trove of experiences. But that is often deeply buried in the past. We have forgotten how many pitfalls we have overcome or at least survived, and, most of all, how we did it. We can retrieve the treasure by examining our life experiences closely. My personal treasure trove of life experiences has made it possible for me not only to cope with the most recent crisis, but to turn it into an *opportunity* in the best sense of the word.

Find Your Treasure of Life Experiences

For more than four years, I had been a successful company director—and it had been fulfilling work. But the one hundred-year-old company was on the brink of a major change. New investors came on board and a new CEO took over the operations from the owner. He pushed forward an ambitious project to restructure the whole company. At the beginning of 2018, I learned that my position as a director would probably be axed. My responsibilities would be split into two departments, and strategically this made sense. But on a personal level, it pushed my family and me into a deep crisis. My job prospects were uncertain, yet as the breadwinner, I had financial responsibility for my family. A year previously, we had welcomed our first child, and the second was on the way. We had just bought a house and had financial obligations.

The uncertain future, the pressure at work, and the responsibility at home left their marks. More and more often, I lay awake at night and ruminated. Then I suddenly did what had helped me during my kidnapping: I began to write down my thoughts, putting all my worries and fears on paper, unfiltered. I poured it all out. "When I lose my job ... we have to sell the house, I will have to do a badly paid and stressful job or to look nationwide, and we will have to move again. I won't have any more time for my family, and that would be bad for our relationship, and ...

and … and …" After a while it clicked. I realized that I had been in a similarly hopeless situation several times before and had wrestled with similarly destructive thoughts. And so far, I had always landed on my feet. This simple realization gave me my first wave of confidence.

The first step toward retrieving a treasure trove of life experiences is to locate where it is stored. "You have to find it first!" The search starts with the question "What crises have I survived in my life so far?" As the journey into the past can be quite challenging, it's advisable to seek some support. Tell yourself that you are a resilient person at this very moment. You have overcome quite a few low points in your life and survived. That's good to know. But it can also be helpful to set out on this treasure hunt in the company of a good mate. By this I mean that the discovery and processing of possibly traumatic experiences shouldn't be undertaken alone, but rather accompanied by a therapist.

How do we actually recognize a crisis? The trigger is clearly defined after a traumatic event like a bereavement, a serious illness, a catastrophe, or an accident, but it's more difficult when a crisis creeps up on you. Events such as burnouts, breakups, or bankruptcy are mostly the result of slower developments. Whether or not someone is mentally thrown off track by a sudden event varies from case to case. I know people who, after being dismissed from their job, crowed, "Super! I'm delighted about the severance pay!" but are maybe devastated by every minor ailment.

Others consider a breakup as a chance to live their life to the full but collapse after the smallest change at work. No one is always resilient. Everyone is sometimes more, sometimes less resilient, depending on the challenges facing them.

It's amazing how many life crises you find when you start looking for them, and I heard of so many in various self-help groups or coaching seminars I attended. I sometimes have the feeling that my own life has consisted of a series of serious setbacks, but I've realized that I'm not alone in that. Even better was the realization that, with every crisis I had mastered, I had become more and more serene. I felt that life had steeled me. Scientists call this phenomenon the "steeling" effect. The American researcher Mark Seery conducted an internet poll in which he discovered that people who had coped with three or four serious negative events in their past were mentally healthier than the people who had experienced only one, or who had never experienced a serious setback. That's encouraging!

It seems that we get more and more serene and relaxed with increasing life experience. So, should we just stick it out, grow old, and go through a few more crises? Not necessarily. I believe that you can speed up the process of gaining inner maturity by thoroughly exploiting the full potential of past experiences. This means you need to find access to the treasure trove of life experiences, even if you've consciously buried or forgotten them.

Retrieve the Treasure of Your Life Experiences

When I was lying awake during my most recent crisis, I became aware that I had coped with many other challenges before this impending job loss. I reflected on how I had managed before and, primarily, what I had learned from that experience. I was lucky that I didn't have to start again from scratch. I had been to many self-development workshops and already knew the answers to some of the crucial questions. How did you survive the crisis? What had helped you? What strengths do you have that you can also retrieve in the future?

I knew that I had many resources and abilities that had helped me in critical situations before. I consciously reflected on those and, bit by bit, gained courage and confidence. Those resources and abilities included:

- *Social support*: My family and friends are always behind me in an emergency.
- *Initiative*: I have always found a new well-paid job.
- *Resilience*: I have always gained more strength from my crises. The owl experience and the kick in the butt led to a leadership position.
- *Flexibility*: I'm an expert on the subject of moving to a new house and my wife is even better.
- *Willingness to learn*: I find it easy to adapt to a new job. I'm good at projects.

- *Network*: I have many job opportunities because of my professional contacts.
- *Humor*: If nothing else works, my gallows humor always helps.

The last point, humor, didn't show up at first. I didn't feel like laughing at all. But a few days later, my wife and I were able to have a good laugh about the whole miserable situation. We did a brainstorming session on a few flip-chart sheets in our living room. "What should we do when Marc loses his job?" We had quite a few crazy ideas. "Travel the world to find new inspiration." "Marc sets up with a guitar and a hat in the town center." "We become self-sufficient in the campervan." But we also wrote down more serious ideas like "coaching" or "training."

When I went back to work, I felt more detached. In contrast to my burnout phase at Renault, I was conscious that I was now free. I could leave if I had to. I'm not a hostage to my job. I observed, with my newly found inner objectivity, how the company was developing and what this meant for me. For months on end my career was very uncertain, but again my motto was "keep your head!" I remained optimistic by believing in a happy ending. At the same time, I developed a Plan B. My resource network helped me in that.

I had considered the idea of taking up coaching for a while, but so far hadn't gone into detail of what that would mean. A friend of mine named Sebastian Mauritz, who is an expert in resilience, helped me by asking the right questions, such as "When do your eyes light up?" I told him enthusiastically how positively I regarded my current crisis; that it seemed to contain opportunity; that I had resurrected my "keep your head" motto from the time in the jungle; and that I would like to share this with other people. We very quickly came to the conclusion that my top driver at the moment had a name: it was *resilience*. Sebastian invited me to one of his workshops with the words "Maybe you'd like to become a trainer in resilience yourself?"

At work, suddenly another door opened. There was the prospect of a new job, running part of my former department. I weighed it. On the one hand, there was the potential for security and a good salary. That was attractive, and probably the best for our family. We could keep the house in Göttingen and carry on as before. On the other hand, the new position felt like a step back on the career ladder, among other factors, but that wasn't very important to me. I would have to split the areas of training and treatment, which in recent years I had merged after much effort and complications. Most of all, though, I resented something else. The company was planning to float on the stock market, and this meant that I was dealing more with numbers again and not with concepts. I found less and less time for serious conversations with my colleagues and clients, and that would only get worse in the future.

The prospect of again being a prisoner to numbers and

figures triggered the old signs of stress. I didn't sleep well, my heart worked overtime, I was sweating, and my eyelids started to twitch. Luckily, I had mostly retrieved my treasure trove of life experiences in my personal development seminars and workshops and knew what question would help me now. "In what part of your body do you feel that you're under stress?"

I knew the harbingers of burnout, the so-called somatic markers. There was a time when I had tried to reduce stress by doing sport and meditation. But I knew that it wouldn't be enough now because I would only fight the symptoms rather than find their roots. I had done that at Renault—had tried to stick at it rather than make a decision. *Leave it, love it, or change it.* My body then had made the decision for me: *leave it.* I'm very grateful to my body for that, because without those signals, I would still be slaving away for eighty hours a week, instead of doing something that I really like.

It's a common mistake to believe that resilient people can withstand everything. With resilience, it's not about reducing stress, because stress is an important signal to implement changes. Truly resilient people don't only try to reduce their stress, but also to ask themselves what it is trying to tell them. They look for its origins and try to find a cure. Stress is like a smoke alarm. When it starts beeping, it gets on your nerves, and after a while it really hurts your ears. But no one would ever dream of dismantling the smoke alarm or taking the batteries out. What if there is a fire somewhere? The solution is to extinguish it. But you would never remove the smoke alarm!

Would you recognize your smoke alarm? We all have different signals for stress. One person might develop sleeping problems, another might drink more. There are headaches, stomachaches, skin problems, high blood pressure, teeth-grinding at night, dizziness, etc. How do you know that something is not right? That there is a fire? I have learned to consider my stress reactions as friends in an emergency. That doesn't mean I've become a stress junkie or someone who runs away at the slightest sign of stress. But I look very closely whether it's worthwhile to tolerate the stress—or not.

In my view, there are two kinds of crises—those you have to stick out, meaning getting up and carrying on, and those that make you stop, think, and change. When I was a hostage, I clearly had to stick it out. There weren't any decisions I could make. I could neither learn to love the jungle nor leave it, nor could I change the situation fundamentally.

But in most situations in life, we are physically free and can make a decision. We often wrongly feel like hostages to our job, our finances, our relationships. Certainly, sometimes there are serious dependencies. But when your health is at stake, it's often the lesser evil to take a courageous step—as opposed to a terrible end and then endless terror. When the smoke alarm starts beeping, it's time to make a decision before your body does it for you.

Stress is the little brother of a crisis. Both can be important signposts for you to make imminent changes. It doesn't have to be a big crisis that forces a change. Sometimes it's enough to take stress as a portent for a crisis. But all too often we overlook those omens. That's not surprising, because very often we hear in difficult times, "Close your eyes and get through it." But it's often the smarter alternative to keep your eyes open. Looking at the mood barometer in a relationship can help you realize that a thunderstorm is imminent. A final breakup often announces itself through arguments, estrangement, affairs, etc. But many people need a big crisis before they wake up, even when it's about their own health. Slight complaints are ignored; a bad backache is treated with painkillers. You have to carry on, people think, until a disc gives way. At work, this time I had heard my smoke alarm and took a courageous decision: *leave it.*

Build Up the Treasure Trove of Your Life Experiences

Leaving the company wasn't only a decision to move *away* from it, especially as I had spent ten successful years there, five in a fulfilling leadership role. It was a decision "toward" something as well—entering a completely new world of working. The idea to become a freelance coach with emphasis on resilience had grown to be more and more attractive to me. Before, I probably would never have dared to take this courageous step from secure employment into the freelance life, but I used the crisis as a push toward self-realization. Everyone grows with his or her tasks. For five years, I had grown toward leadership, at work and privately. In the end, it nearly felt like a comfort zone. But in 2019, I left it in many ways. For one thing, my family responsibilities had grown. I was gifted with a second child. The other thing was that I had laid the foundation for self-employment. But that whole year still felt like building a nest while in free flight—a challenging combination, and I was highly grateful for my well-developed resilience.

Being self-employed means that there's no financial security at all, something I had been used to in employment. For the first time in my life, there were no external structures—no boss, no financial security, no safety net. It was like jumping into the cold, big pool again. Previously, I would have avoided these kinds of risks. But now I consider this chance to have been a gift. I can do whatever I like. And as I know what I want, I do it with joy and energy. I can write a book about all the things that have been close to my heart for years. I can hold talks and carry my message to others. I can train people to cope with their crises and hardships with strength. I feel fulfilled every time someone gives me feedback that I have been able to inspire them.

My talents and desires have come together in my new

profession as if someone has waved a magic wand. My work really feels like a calling and not like a job. In hindsight, all my life crises make profound sense and have built my treasure trove of experiences. Life has made me an expert in resilience. During my training as a resilience coach, I was glad to find how valuable my own experiences are in this area. Everything fits now. Even my seventeen years in the corporate world suddenly make complete sense.

My experience in the jungle helped me time and again in the corporate world, particularly when I was responsible for a team. Today, I can pass on what I learned in my leadership roles and when I was a hostage to other organizations via talks and training seminars.

These days, I consciously increase my treasure trove of life experiences by sharing them and thus refining them. Knowledge based on experience grows when it is shared, just like love and happiness do. You have to make your own experiences, but you can also learn from those of other people, particularly the painful experiences. During the last few years, I have explored my treasure trove of life experiences, found most of them, and retrieved them. I have clarified what adventures I had already lived through and coped with, what strengths I had used and developed further. During the process, I became more aware of myself and I developed self-confidence. Today, I'm less frightened of future unpredictability and challenges because I know I can cope with them, as I have done so often in the past. That's worth a lot, but it's no reason to stand still. Quite the opposite.

You can train yourself to be resilient, but it's also easy to forget everything you've learned. You slacken if you stay too long in your comfort zone, like an athlete losing stamina when resting on his or her laurels. It's important therefore to leave your comfort zone time and again to train your "resilience muscles," to strengthen them or at least stay fit. It takes quite a bit of effort, and I regularly force myself to leave my comfort zone.

In the morning, I take a hot shower because I like it, and then turn the tap to cold because it makes me stronger. Before I switch on the cold tap, I tell myself, "Get out of your comfort zone, life is waiting!" This little ritual gives me a boost to tackle the day ahead, and I'm ready for the next challenge. I went through a harder version of this ritual during the difficult phase of my self-development. I did extreme running events whose names—"Braveheart Battle," "Getting Tough," etc.—told the story. The runs are longer than a half-marathon and also have hurdles—and they were about the last thing I fancied at the time, but I pushed myself and eventually got used to them. With time, I found it a bit easier to leave my comfort zone in everyday life as well. I also learned to make some uncomfortable decisions and see them through.

In life, everything eventually changes. There's a saying that life is a river you never get into twice. When you stop changing, sooner or later you will be forced to by a crisis.

I've grasped that now. These days, my life plan is to consciously aim for constant growth outside my comfort zone. My life contains continuous changes and challenges. My relationship reflects this, because it's not cozy and calm, but challenging and lively. I've gone freelance, and pursue my work with courage. Both changes, in my marriage and my work, I probably wouldn't have dared to do if I hadn't retrieved my treasure trove of life experiences. From now on, I'll guard it well and add to it too.

Inspiration

Crises are a part of life. We can't prevent them. But we can steel ourselves for them. We can aim to retrieve our treasure trove of life experiences and use it in future challenges. For this, the following questions might help: "What crisis have I coped with before? What has helped me? We can add to this trove of life experiences by leaving our comfort zone and consciously planning changes in our life. And we can share our experiences, because it will enhance them—just like love and happiness.

STRONG IN A CRISIS AS A TEAM

My exceptional experience of being kidnapped and held hostage maps surprisingly well to everyday challenges of teams and organizations. I have seen this time and again during my corporate career. The challenges in the Philippine jungle and in the business jungle are basically the same. Both are full of uncertainty and stress.

You can use jungle strategies as a guide when answering the following business-related questions. What makes a team strong and flexible in times of uncertainty and rapid change? What attitude helps in times of major and disruptive change such as digitalization?

How to Turn a Group into a Team

I've often been asked whether our group of hostages worked together as a team or whether we had many conflicts. The answer is ... both. Togetherness and conflicts aren't mutually exclusive. In a way, they are mutually dependent. A group grows into a successful team not in spite of its constructive conflicts, but because of them.

The success of a group is not measured by its level of harmony, but whether it reaches its target. And we achieved our goal 100 percent. All twenty-one hostages survived. Without teamwork, including the conflicts, it would probably not have been possible. There's no teamwork without teambuilding, no teambuilding without conflicts. In a way, I have to laugh at myself about how strongly I'm advocating for conflicts now. Me! I used to think "What a waste of time and energy conflicts are! Maybe in the end the relationship or the team will fall apart! What if we never make up again?" That was the spiral of anxious thoughts swirling around my head whenever there was a conflict brewing or when an argument became emotional. I've always tried my very best to stifle conflicts by employing diplomacy at the very first signs. I stopped getting lost in fearful thoughts only after I came to understand that conflicts aren't a bad thing. They are like a cleansing thunderstorm. This insight has benefited not only my private life, but also my career.

In corporate organizations, it's often necessary to form interdisciplinary teams to tackle complex challenges, be it the introduction of a new product or the change of internal procedures by new software. In such situations, it helps to know that one cannot avoid conflicts during the project altogether, and when under pressure of deadlines, they are practically programmed in. When you bear in mind that conflicts contribute to solutions in an interdisciplinary team, then you are well prepared to keep your head in the heat of the battle.

I only understood that properly when I dealt with the issue of teambuilding in a leadership role. In hindsight, my kidnapping offered valuable experience in terms of group dynamics and conflict management. I want to illustrate the wisdom I gained at that time. Here are some helpful ideas on this important topic.

Inspiration

The art of keeping your head as a team means to consciously deal with conflicts and consider them a necessary process in the development of the group. It means that you shouldn't get sidetracked by feelings of animosity but should always keep your eye on the solutions. What can we learn from this conflict? Conflicts should be brought up and discussed openly. Only then they can be constructive, and the team will grow by coping with the crisis.

Survival in Extreme Conditions

If you took away the hostage situation, the conditions in the jungle were in some ways like in a dream I had often had as a stressed-out manager. There were no appointments, no phone, and no internet. We were on a most beautiful tropical island, surrounded by unspoiled nature—including monkeys in the trees—enjoying all-day sunshine together with people from all corners of the world who were united by their love of diving. Sounds amazing, doesn't it? But the reality was different.

For months, we were subjected to the following stress factors, each of which on their own could ordinarily have triggered a serious crisis:

- *Uncertainty*: We never knew what would happen next or whether we would survive.
- *Mortal danger*: We were threatened with decapitation, military attacks, diseases, injuries, and poisonous insects.
- *Culture shock*: As a trainer in interculturalism, I had prepared people for stays abroad, also for an inevi-

table culture shock. After the initial phase of being abroad, when someone is bursting with energy because everything is new and strange, what often follows is a phase of exhaustion that can express itself as aggression or depression. On Jolo, we hadn't only ended up deep in an Asian rainforest, but also in a war zone in a culture of fighting. To top that, our group consisted of people from seven countries who spoke eight languages. That alone led to several misunderstandings because everyone interpreted words, gestures, and facial expressions differently, according to their values. After a while, that can get on your nerves.

– *No privacy*: For months, we lived in each other's pockets without the slightest chance of privacy. We hostages could hardly ever avoid each other. Additionally, we were constantly being watched by our guards. But there were also daily visits by civilians from the nearby villages to stare at the strange white men. How much we longed for a bit of solitude! But that wasn't even possible on the toilet. I could never have guessed how much that would bother me.

– *Survival in the jungle*: During our time as hostages, the reality show *Das Inselduell* (*The Island Duel,* based on the American show *Survivor*) started filming nearby. Over seven weeks, viewers watched thirteen contestants fighting for survival on an island in Malaysia. The contestants were well-equipped with mosquito nets, a first aid kit was always within reach, and a helicopter ambulance could be called by one of their emergency phones. The survival tasks were, among other things, to catch an escaped chicken or collect mussels. We, however, had to deal with real threats, such as mosquitoes that could transmit malaria or dengue fever, black mambas, spiders as big as your hand, and poisonous scorpions. One of the Asian hostages was bitten by a scorpion and suffered a fever for several days. Our medical supplies consisted mainly of painkillers.

- *Malnutrition*: We usually had less than a liter of drinking water per day—in a tropical climate in which we were all sweating profusely. As for food, in the first few weeks, we only had rice, and sometimes only a small portion, which was often burnt. Every now and then, we received a tin of sardines to share between us—getting only a tiny bit each. I can confirm that, when people are hungry, conflicts about the distribution of food are inevitable.
- *Hygiene*: There are no toilets in the rainforest. The rainforest is the toilet. The hostages, as well as the rebels, constantly had to look for new places to relieve themselves. After a few days, the ground around the camp was littered with "landmines," often teeming with worms in all shapes and colors. Wearing flip flops, and often in the dark, we really

had to watch our steps. And after a tropical rainstorm, everything became flooded with it. In the first few weeks, we wiped ourselves with dried banana leaves. There was hardly ever any water to wash our hands. Additionally, most of us were suffering from diarrhea, which makes it understandable that in this area we all quickly reached our limits.

Considering the circumstances, it is remarkable that there was never any violence among us. It would have been a miracle if there hadn't been any conflicts—and that would have been a risk, because without conflicts no team spirit can develop.

A Group Becomes a Team

A group of people isn't necessarily a team that can function toward a common goal. A team only becomes successful and performs well when it has passed through certain phases and processes. And conflicts are a necessary part of it.

In 1965, Bruce Tuckman, an American psychologist, developed the so-called "phase model" of team building that to this day is considered the gold standard in organizational psychology. Groups go through four or five stages of development, each of which is crucial for its performance as a team as well as its atmosphere. It's interesting that according to Tuckman, every group will pass through the four phases if they are together long enough and have a common goal. It wouldn't apply to a group of travelers on a train who have hardly any contact with each other and no common goal apart from their destination. But the phases are valid for any team that has to resolve a task in a given time. And, of course, they are valid for people who have been kidnapped and have to spend one hundred forty days in the jungle.

The model simplifies the complex interpersonal processes that happen in the real world—be it the corporate world or the jungle. But it still gives us a solid understanding of the dynamics in groups and the formation of a team. The necessity of conflicts for the performance of the group can be directly deduced from it. The model enables executives, project managers, and team members—all those who lead a group or belong to one—to purposefully manage the necessary processes.

These are the phases:

1. *Forming* (contact): This is the orientation phase, in which the members of the group get to know one another. It's normally characterized by curiosity, politeness, and openness toward the other members of the group, but also by insecurity, reticence, or even confusion. The relationship of the group members to each other and their position within the group are still vague.

2. *Storming* (conflict): This is the phase of close combat. There are conflicts about the roles, the prioritizing of goals, and the methods of working. There is no chance of productive cooperation during this phase. There are fights for superiority, and the atmosphere is tense and sometimes hostile. First agreements begin to emerge.
3. *Norming* (contract): This is the organizational phase, in which clear structures and agreements are reached. Rules and rituals are established, either formally or non-verbally. The roles are clearly allocated, and the atmosphere gets more harmonious and cooperative. The focus is on moving toward the task at hand.
4. *Performing* (cooperation): This is the integration phase, in which the team operates autonomously. During this phase, the team is constantly capable of achieving common agreements and aims. The atmosphere is positive, trustful, and supportive. The work is solution-focused and carried out flexibly and cooperatively. Reaching this phase is the aim of the team-building process.
5. *Adjourning* (dissolving): Not all teams go through the goodbye phase, and it is only a possible add-on to the four core phases. The fifth phase is relevant for teams that will dissolve after achieving a common goal, that is, they will return to everyday functions. It's frequently shaped by grief and worry about the time after the team dissolves. This phase

offers itself as time for an intense discussion about "lessons learned."

No team goes through all five phases in a strict order, and it's also not possible to predict how long each phase will take. The phases are often fluid and run into each other and vary in length. Some groups seem to skip whole phases or never get to them. A group's homogeneity, or its similarity, is a crucial factor. The more similar the members are, the faster they go through the phases and the more harmonious the "group feeling" becomes. That makes sense. The more similar the members are, the fewer conflict issues arise. But a high level of homogeneity or low heterogeneity (that is, dissimilarity) within the group has a strong negative impact on the performance of the group, because the group has less variety of competencies.

Reverting to an earlier phase is also quite common. It means that the whole process starts again from scratch when something changes within the group, like a new member joining or a member leaving. Usually the re-formed group goes through the phases faster than the first time, but the basic process remains the same.

This restart of the cycle also happens in stable teams after they achieve a task and when they start a new project. It means that, with each new task, the same team can go through the four phases again—and conflict precedes performance.

In my long experience as a project manager and executive, I know that team conflicts don't enjoy a good reputation in the world of business. Often, they are rejected as creating a "bad atmosphere" instead of being appreciated as helpful clarifications. Many executives shy away from conflicts and don't openly deal with them. They tend to stifle discussions or belittle them. Of course, conflicts cost energy. But the phase model clearly shows how important the fight about boundaries, status, and agreements is in a group, especially in order to achieve a high functioning level as a team.

The group dynamics we achieved in our jungle group, as we changed from a mixed group of international hostages to a successful team, can be easily followed along the lines of those phases. Our story shows clearly how valuable the difficult conflict phases were for team building.

A Bunch of People Thrown Together by Fate — Forming

On April 23, 2000, twenty-one people accidentally became companions in a fateful adventure. We only knew each other fleetingly from the diving excursions or from seeing each other in the restaurant. But from one moment to the next, we were all suddenly in the same boat literally—well, in two boats. After twenty hours, we landed on the Philippine island of Jolo and, in a bamboo hut, we introduced ourselves to each other, partly in broken English, partly with gestures.

For the first time, we got an idea of what kind of a motley crew we were: twenty-one people from seven countries, between twenty and fifty-seven years of age, with a variety of occupations.

There were three Germans—me, then twenty-six years old, a management consultant in Luxembourg; my father Werner, fifty-seven, a geography teacher; and my mother Renate, fifty-six, a music teacher.

Two Finns—Risto, forty-eight, an engineer and manager; and Seppo, fifty, a nurse and an artist.

Two South Africans—Monique, thirty-six, an actor; and Callie, thirty-seven, a key account manager.

Three French—Stéphane, thirty-four, an engineer; his partner Sonja, thirty-four, an engineer; and Marie, thirty-three, from Lebanon, a marketing manager.

Nine Malaysians—Ken, twenty-seven, a diving instructor; Vincent, forty, a diving instructor; Lee, twenty, a chef; Ah Loong, twenty-four, a chef; Abdul, thirty-nine, a policeman; Hashim, twenty-nine, a wildlife ranger; Francis, thirty-five, a wildlife ranger; Nair, twenty-four, a wildlife ranger; Jim, thirty-one, a wildlife ranger.

Two Filipinos—Abi, forty-one, a wildlife ranger; and Aida, thirty-four, a kitchen manager.

The group immediately began its formation phase. Marie and I, as an invented couple, were the fifth couple apart from Callie and Monique, Stéphane and Sonja, my parents, and the two Finnish friends. Only Aida, the Filipina kitchen manager from our hotel, was single. She joined the group of Western hostages rather than the Asian one to avoid being the only woman among men, and the kidnappers luckily accepted this. I couldn't figure out the makeup of the other ten Asian hostages, because most of the time we were kept in separate places.

During the getting-to-know phase, we were all curious and open. We tried to assess the others' situations. The atmosphere was mostly friendly; everyone was cooperative, apart from some ugly scenes on the boat when we had to share the sparse drinking water. But we were united against a common enemy.

After a ten-hour trek through the jungle, we arrived at the first of seven camps we occupied during our captivity. We were shocked by the state of the bamboo hut that the kidnappers proudly called their "headquarters"—a structure without electricity or running water. Our faces all showed our disappointment about the primitiveness of our accommodation, and we all felt low. Later, though, we would call the place the "Crown Plaza" because in comparison with the other camps it could be called luxurious. At least there was a roof—of corrugated iron!

The kidnappers split us into two groups. The ten tourists and Aida were shown into a more-or-less closed room, together with its regular inhabitant and her baby. The ten Asian hotel employees had to spend the night on the "veranda."

To paint the picture: we were lying like spoons in an area of about twenty square meters, covered in sweat, dirt, and mosquitoes. But in contrast to the Asian hostages, we had a roof over our head and a certain sense of safety.

The Western hostages continuously got preferential treatment from the kidnappers. To them, we were more valuable because they could demand a higher ransom for us. Our Asian companions were treated as second-class hostages from the beginning, and I'm ashamed to say that we never really acted on their behalf either. When sparse resources were distributed, we always gave our own group priority, and our Asian compatriots were slighted or ignored.

Already there was a principle evolving. Separation leads to an "out of sight, out of mind" mentality, while close proximity strengthens the team spirit. Being housed together had a strong influence on us as a group. When, after a month, we arrived at our sixth camp, the rebels built two bamboo sleeping platforms for us and put a plastic sheet over it to give us shelter from the rain. That was the first time our group of Western hostages was split up. There were only a few meters between the two platforms, but it felt much wider. The Finns, French, my parents, and I were on one platform, the South Africans, Marie, and Aida on the other. In the dead of night, things happened in two parallel worlds. If someone had a bad night owing to pain or nightmares, we only heard about it the next morning.

Without a doubt, every one of us would have appreciated a bit more space and privacy. On the other hand, the group situation demanded a lot of dynamic closeness. Knowing exactly how the other ones were and the informal exchange of information would have gotten lost otherwise to be replaced by more formal communication.

As a group of eleven, we were in a good place to cooperate as a team; it was just the right number, not too many, not too few.

The behavioral biologist Konrad Lorenz considered a group of eleven as ideal, like in a primeval tribe where each member still could see, hear, and smell the others, which would ensure cohesion against hostile attacks. In our case, the lack of space did indeed increase the cohesion, but also again and again it challenged us, because we heard each other snore, could smell each other's sweat, and see each other urinate. In a sense, we lived like a primeval tribe. It wasn't easy at all, but we didn't really have a choice.

As we were separated from the Asian hostage group for most of the time, the following information on the group dynamics mainly applies to the group of the ten Western hostages plus Aida.

Insights

Physical closeness of people has advantages and disadvantages, but one thing is certain, it plays an important role in team building. For that reason, organizations experiment with concepts of space, from single offices, to open plan or co-working spaces, looking for the optimal mixture of concentrated seclusion and creative exchange. As an executive, I've spent a lot of time on this issue in order to smoothly coordinate my seven departments in three different locations.

Lots of Conflicts (Storming)

In the jungle, we argued about a lot of things that in normal life we didn't even think about because we took them for granted—water, food, space, fire, paper, pencils, plastic bags, and many other things.

Resources vital for our survival were scarce. We Western hostages especially had been ripped out of our normal materialistic comfort zone. But much worse was that we lost our freedom and control over our lives. We had to switch to survival mode—one in which we not only reached our personal limits but also those of our fellow sufferers. As we approached those limits, we had conflicts time and again.

Dear God, Give Us Some Water!

Ironically, although we were in the middle of a rainforest, water was amazingly scarce. But in the humid climate, one needs a lot of drinking water to survive. We would sweat just sitting in one place. So, we had to drink a lot to avoid dehydration. Bodily hygiene was equally important. After only a few days, some of us had an inflammation in delicate regions. In the first camp, we were cut off from water for nearly a week, as the Philippine military had surrounded the camp and blocked access to nearby water sources. Our water supply was restricted to sporadic deliveries in old petrol cans. The water, of course, tasted of petrol, and when we poured it into a different container, we discovered tadpoles in it. Still, we were very thirsty and lapped it up. And if one of us became greedy and drank more than his share or even wanted to wash his dirty hands and feet, we argued about the fair distribution of this scarce resource. The mood among us became more aggressive then.

But the mood lifted considerably after the first tropical downpour—at that point it was a veritable gift from God. It was gushing down and created a very welcome opportunity for a shower, to wash one's whole body for once. We jumped around on our veranda like children, shouting with joy. The rebels and civilians around us found this very funny. You could see in their faces what they were thinking: "Those white people are crazy!" But then we were told off because we had stripped down to our underwear and had violated a taboo in the otherwise tolerant Islamic island culture. Our mood dropped when we were reminded again of our precarious reality, but at least we felt clean for the first time.

Only Rice — and Not Enough of It

After a few days on Jolo, Soraya arrived. She was the cousin of one of the rebel leaders, and took on the role of chef. She had a large pot and a big spoon and prepared two to three meals a day. In other words—she boiled rice. It was served on banana leaves, and we ate with our fingers, sitting on the ground. That diet was a big change for the spoiled tourists. But sometimes it got even worse, when the rice was burnt because there hadn't been enough water for boiling it. Sometimes there wasn't even rice because the supply had been captured by the military. Especially in the beginning of our group experience, hunger became an unpleasant companion and a big challenge for us. When the first aid delivery arrived, we each got an orange frisbee as a plate and a fork.

In hindsight, it's amazing that the difficult supply situation didn't lead to violence among us. There were conflicts and arguments when the food was being distributed, and they were resolved only later. But before that happened, another delivery of aid made us more relaxed. After about two weeks, we got a few battle rations from the French military. The Western hostages practically jumped onto the biscuits and soups; our Asian fellow sufferers didn't get anything. It was felt that they were not part of our team, kept away from us and in any case were more modest, long suffering, and used to eating only rice—that's what we told ourselves most egocentrically. For me, it's one of the parts in our involuntary group experiment I'm not proud of.

No Roof Above Our Heads

Twice, the Philippine military wanted to demonstrate its power and attacked our kidnappers who were using us as human shields. We had to flee our first camp in a hurry and later changed our hideaways in the jungle several more times. Other than in the "Crown Plaza," the accommodations didn't have a roof, and we slept on the ground or an open bamboo platform, exposed to the weather and the mosquitoes.

When a German aid package arrived containing two plastic survival bags to protect us from the nightly drop in temperature, we quickly agreed that we wouldn't use the bags for only two people but as a sheet to protect us all from the rain. Rain can be a blessing if you can go to a dry space afterwards. But if you have to spend the night soaking wet, there's not only the danger of cooling down too much, but the risk of mold developing on your skin.

In the second camp, our roof sheet wasn't big enough to give everyone shelter from the regular rainfall. With a sense of irony, we christened this place "Open-Air Camp." We could all stay dry, but only from above, by sitting closely together. On the ground, the water soaked everything.

So, there was a fight for the scarce resource of a dry sleeping place. We discussed how to share it as fairly as possible, and somehow, we all slept, but no one was really happy with the situation, because of the many possibilities and perceptions of what was fair. Who should have the best places? Ladies first? Or rather the weaker and sick people? Those who had constructed the roof? Or the ones who had gone without before?

We got to know each other very well during those conflicts, all our weaknesses, our needs, our qualities, and strengths. This contributed a lot to becoming a very strong team.

Arguments About the "Luxury Items"

During the first weeks, the conflicts in the group were mainly about basic physical needs. With every delivery by our embassies or relatives, our situation got better. But it's interesting that the atmosphere in the group didn't improve, it rather deteriorated for a while. A battle started about the small luxury items that could enhance one's sense of wellbeing. Emotional stability was just as important in our situation as physical stability. Both were essential for our survival.

Some of the later camps were situated near little rivers. We didn't have to ask anymore whether we *could* wash, but for how long. In one place, there was even a bamboo pipe delivering fresh spring water. But the times for an idyllic jungle shower were limited, because with each foray outside the camp we were in danger of being attacked by the military or a rival rebel group. As a result, we were always accompanied by armed "bodyguards" and told to hurry. But we couldn't stay too long near the river anyway because of the aggressive swarms of mosquitoes. So, there was a conflict about the shower. We all would have loved to stay under the bamboo pipe for ten minutes, for once unmolested by mosquitoes, and to enjoy the fresh water and a moment of peace. This little escape from the arduous jungle life was very important psychologically. But not so for the ones waiting. "Get on with it!" "Me next!" "I'm getting bitten to death here!" were the shouts from the queue to the one who was just enjoying his shower.

The argument about the satellite phone was quite a strange experience. Yes, we had a satellite phone! At least for one day in May. Some journalists offered us their phone to ring home. The rush for it was immense. My mother soaked up every word of my brother and, for a moment, could forget everything around her. I rang a friend and could finally describe our situation from our point of view without the interpretations and slant of journalists. We didn't think about what those phone calls did emotionally to the people at the other end; what counted for us was the incredibly precious connection to home. Some people completely lost their sense of time when it was their turn. Seppo couldn't stop ringing people and got so absorbed talking to home that the battery ran out. Understandably, the ones who had been waiting for their turn were very cross.

Minor items such as plastic bags, pens, and paper also led to arguments. The numerous journalists who came to see and interview us during our captivity often gave us those useful things. They enabled us to keep a diary and write letters, to express our experiences in drawings and process them. Whoever had pen and paper was at an advantage. If you then also had a plastic bag to protect everything from the rain, you were king. And those who only had a bad pen or a piece of carton were envious, and when you only once had experienced your writings or drawings being irretrievably destroyed by a rain shower, you weren't very tolerant toward those who used their many plastic bags to store their wellies.

The better supplied we were with everyday items, the more we argued about them. It was much less now about the question "What do I need for survival?" but increasingly about "Do the others have more than I do?" It was just as back in normal day-to-day life when you feel disadvantaged because your neighbor has a bigger car or your colleague has a private office.

The conflicts in our group resulted from the fear for one's own survival but were also rooted in envy and perceived unfairness. Resentful discussions and arguments about trivial things can be fairly annoying, but they are human. And as long as those quarrels don't carry on endlessly but can be resolved, in the long run they even contribute to the team-building process. Bruce Tuckman describes the normative power of conflicts in the Third Phase of the team-building process. Luckily, we went through this phase in the jungle—time and time again.

Inspiration

Arguments about the allocation of resources are common in team conflicts. But they need a closer look as to whether they are about a sensible distribution of team resources toward a common goal, or are degenerating into a "me, me, me" quarrel. Organizational measures help with the sharing of resources, and when unfairness is perceived, mediation helps.

We Became a Team — Despite or Because of the Conflicts (*Norming*)

We didn't only resolve conflicts within the group, but also used them for establishing common norms, agreements, and rituals, as illustrated in the following examples.

After a time, most of us were angry at Seppo. He even had a nickname, "The Taker," because he frequently helped himself to more than he was due—longer showers, the longest call on the satellite phone, or the best sleeping place. His behavior was considered selfish and was punished by angry reproaches or being ignored. In the fourth week, his compatriot Risto called for a meeting. All eleven hostages sat down in the flickering light of a candle. Risto opened the discussion in his fluent English with the confidence of a CEO—which he was in real life. He said, "The tension within the group has increased recently, and Seppo is suffering from the rejection by the group. I'm asking for your understanding and your consideration. Not everyone can handle a situation such as this one, in which we are all together, in the same way. Seppo is terribly frightened of death and in his misery requires more comforting and needs your support. He is sorry that he sometimes appears greedy, but he can't help it. He also finds it difficult to integrate as his English is not very good." Spontaneously, some of us got up and hugged Seppo, which nearly made him cry. Then the whole group sang "Happy Birthday" to him—it was the only song we all knew the lyrics to. The French hostages donated a "Peace Pizza" they had been given by some French journalists. Not only was the mood in the group suddenly on a high, this also established a norm: "Some of us are weaker than others and need more help and resources." Before, there had been an unwritten rule: "We are all in the same boat, and everybody gets an equal share."

The Impact of Money

It might sound crazy, but at some point, we got hold of some money—in the middle of the jungle! Some journalists had given us some pesos as a goodbye present, not as a thank you for the interviews, but seriously meant as support. And we indeed could buy some items and food and thus improve our standard of living considerably. Amazingly, it was tolerated by our kidnappers. We were allowed to keep the money and use it as we liked.

The French journalists were the first to donate money, and, of course, the French hostages were the first to receive it. Most of us only learned about it by chance, when the French and a few chosen ones were suddenly standing at the "kiosk" in the jungle, a cola in their hand. The local population wanted to benefit from the hostage tourism of the journalists, organized soft drinks and sweets from the nearby village, and offered it at improvised bamboo stalls. A warm soft drink isn't exactly the bee's knees, but it is a taste experience that for a few moments catapults you back to civilization, so in that respect is not to be underestimated as a psychological hit.

It wasn't the first case of an unfair distribution of resources. Nearly everyone had at some point kept part of the aid delivery from their embassy or journalists for themselves. But with money, the unfairness had reached a new dimension. Now it wasn't only about the fair sharing of resources, but on what we would spend the money and what were the priorities.

Again, there were heated discussions along the lines of the nationality of the money owners and the non-money owners. It wasn't nice, but nevertheless, it was cleansing. Because we agreed to make a large part of the money collective property and to spend it on basic foodstuffs and equipment. That meant vegetables, fish, and soap for everyone, instead of cola and sweets for a few. This improved not only the supply situation, but also greatly improved the atmosphere. Every few days, we made a list of things needed and gave it, with the necessary money, to some civilians—rebel sympathizers—who visited us in the camp and could organize the items in the nearby market.

Our agreement about the pooling of the money didn't always work, particularly when it was running out, but at least we had agreed on a rule we could return to in later discussions. The mere existence of a rule is an important and helpful step on the path from a group toward a team.

Roles, Rituals, and a Shared Daily Structure

There were some minor disputes about how to fairly share the daily chores. But in time, rituals, roles, and structures developed that made daily life in the jungle much easier. Smaller groups of three or four, mostly consisting of two nationalities, worked on making the daily water supply more efficient, because the steep path to the water source was slippery, difficult, and sometimes dangerous. In turn, two others went off to wash the clothes, plates, and cutlery for this small group and to get fresh drinking water. This job sharing was successful and a real relief.

Others took on tasks for the whole group, like ordering the foodstuffs, cooking, serving the food, and the storage and distribution of medicines. This role sharing wasn't only easier than doing it separately, it was also an expression of how much trust had developed between us. This boosted the community spirit tremendously.

By now, our daily structure was more or less established, and there were rituals you could rely on and look forward to. I well remember Risto's call every morning when the kettle had boiled. He woke up everyone, shouting, "Cups pleeeeease!" and we all held out our beakers to him to be filled with hot water for tea or instant coffee. The evening ritual of the prayer circle also united a large part of the group, inspired and led by our charismatic mate Callie from South Africa, a devout Christian.

A Common Strategy for Communication

After our first contact with the outside world, we straightaway had a serious conflict within the group. On the seventh day of our captivity, a Philippine journalist turned up and asked: "How do you feel?" In our situation, the question seemed provocative, and I would have loved to answer: "Oh, great! Thank you, we're having a fantastic time!" But here was an opportunity to alert the outside world to our situation and to push for negotiations about our release.

One after the other, we made a dramatic appeal in front of the camera. I said, "My name is Marc Wallert from Göttingen. Please stop all military action and get us out of here as soon as possible!" At some point it was Monique's turn, and she blurted out the silly sentence, "It's not as bad as it seems." This really was less an emotional overreaction than an attempt to reassure her parents.

Well meant, but badly executed was the verdict of the rest of the group. What would they think in the outside world? That everything here wasn't bad at all? That people had all the time in the world to get us out of here? We quickly agreed to leave out statements like that in the future. Instead, we had to point out the seriousness of our situation to put pressure on the ongoing negotiations, by, for example, mentioning my mother's bad physical condition. So, we established norms for the communication to the outside and gave my mother the role as the weakest of the hostages.

When, after three months, we were still in captivity and our appeals felt useless, we changed our strategy. After many ineffective interviews, we decided by majority to stop giving interviews and to ignore the journalists who kept coming. It was a kind of hostage strike. Not that everyone followed this strategy, but the strike-breakers could be sure to attract the anger of the other hostages. My father was one of them.

When that strategy remained unsuccessful, Callie and Monique talked of a hunger strike. The discussion that followed was vehement. Some of us wanted to put pressure on the negotiators, but others found it more appropriate to keep fit and prepare for a possible long stay in the jungle. We didn't come to an agreement, but it was a good discussion with the whole group; one that showed a good deal of tolerance.

But the hunger strike topic concerned the whole group, as time and again, we considered whether to flee, for which we all would have to be absolutely fit. Escaping would only be an option if we did it all together; otherwise, the lives of those left behind would be at risk and exposed to the revenge of the rebels.

Cooperation or Confrontation?

We had to make a fundamental and critical decision about how to deal with our kidnappers. Should we cooperate or be confrontational? Early on we had agreed to build up a good relationship with the kidnappers to raise the emotional threshold for decapitations and abuse. On the boat from Malaysia to the Philippines, they had told us, "You are only our instruments." At first, we thought, okay, they don't object to us personally, that's good. But quickly we realized, if we're only instruments, then they might not hesitate to kill us to get their demands met. We had to try to become individuals to them, not just instruments, and so, began from early on to elicit their sympathy.

Most of us tried to build up a personal relationship with their "bodyguards" whose task was to watch us, look after our security, and prevent us from fleeing. This secured us little everyday advantages, like an extra walk to the water source or information about the negotiations, but most of all it created trust and closeness, so in case of an emergency they might protect us from the other rebels.

This behavior often was wrongly interpreted as an emotional understanding with our kidnappers. The so-called Stockholm syndrome was mentioned, named after a kidnapping situation in Stockholm in 1973 during which some of the hostages emotionally bonded with the kidnappers and defended them after their release. But in our situation, at no point did anyone bond with our kidnappers, rather the opposite. Some of the younger rebels considered me as a role model they adored. They were particularly impressed by my physical height—six foot six—as well as the long scar on my arm. They gave me the nickname Hero or Idol. Sonja had the same experience; with her blonde hair, she embodied an ideal beauty and was particularly admired by the women on the island.

Our cooperative behavior wasn't odd and it wasn't a syndrome, but rather, it was a pragmatic way to deal with the fact that our lives were in the hands of armed people. Luckily, our captors weren't blind with hate, and some of them were helpful and friendly. For example, Mohammad, my mother's bodyguard, transported her on a stretcher over many kilometers through the jungle after her collapse. He also helped her time and again in everyday situations. For example, he reprimanded some younger rebels who, for fun, shot salvoes into the air very close to the camp and triggered a nervous breakdown in my mother.

Mohammad was an experienced fighter of an impressive stature, which made it even more surprising how lovely he was to my mother. When he heard of her release, he cried with joy. But he was also responsible for our life-threatening situation. The world is not only black and white. Any confrontation with our kidnappers would have been highly dangerous. We were shown this in a drastic way when Stéphane lost his nerve. Sihata, the uncle of one of the rebel leaders, one day brought a camera to our camp and started immediately to take photos of us. Stéphane, an impulsive type anyway, was just getting changed. When he noticed Sihata, he shouted at him in anger and made wild gestures. "We aren't animals! Do you understand that?" What followed was a heated discussion, until Sihata ran off to return immediately with a weapon in his hand, shouting, "Do you want to die?"

That evening, we had a long discussion about this critical situation, and in the end agreed. Even if we found it difficult, we had to remain cooperative toward our kidnappers, because they had the stronger arguments—weapons.

Family Structures Upside Down

My own experience of the kidnapping was also shaped by the physical closeness to my parents, something I wasn't used to anymore. In recent years, we had rarely seen each other, as I had moved out after my civil service and then spent the following seven years studying and working abroad. The holidays together had been planned as a reunion, and now it had turned into months of "house sharing," when you couldn't even close a door behind you.

It was an incredibly unique challenge. For my parents, it was particularly stressful because they were not in a position to help me, their son. Quite the opposite—my caring mother now was dependent on her child's help. This reversal of family structures happens sooner or later in most families, but typically stretches over several years. Overnight, however, my mother became an invalid after always previously having been a caring "power woman." My father did most of the work supporting her, since Marie was my "buddy," as you say among divers. But after four weeks, my father too had to take a step back because he had a serious infection with a high temperature following a hand injury.

For me, this meant an additional physical challenge, as

I had to do three water runs in a camp with particularly difficult access to water. It was a mental challenge too to be suddenly responsible for my parents' wellbeing. The whole family structure was upside down, and we only came to terms with it after some difficult moments.

One of those moments was when I got upset about chaos regarding the rice sacks we used for transport. My mother had put an open pack of sugar into the bag with the clothes, which, as a result, was now teeming with ants. So, I took over the organization of our rice sacks. Keeping our few belongings in an orderly way was immensely important for our wellbeing, even though by current standards it would rather look like bags full of waste for recycling.

When my father was fit again, we shared our tasks anew, and my mother too, when she was well, took on small chores in our "household." Time and again we recalibrated the tasks, and within our small group, the dynamics corresponded to the same phases happening in the larger hostage group: *forming, storming, norming, performing.* It was hard work, but it was important and successful in the end. This family experience was difficult, but we were a strong team, just like in freedom—only differently.

The dynamics of the larger group got on our nerves quite often, but in the end, there was always a valuable result for everyone. A good example was the clarification of how we could cooperate with each other in a meaningful way to reach our common goal: "freedom." Today I know that we were such a successful team not despite our conflicts, but because of them.

But not all conflicts within the group were constructive. Some of us simply couldn't stand each other and were constantly irritated. In an informal role as a diplomat, I tried to mediate, but I wasn't impartial after all, and had only limited credibility.

In the corporate world, this would be a classic case for a moderator. As an executive, I once invited an external coach to moderate a team conflict. In the end, the members didn't exactly hug each other, but they all developed an understanding for the perspective and the qualities of the others. And that was helpful. In the jungle, a team workshop with a moderator from the outside also would have been helpful, but that, of course, was out of the question. In the end, we did well as a team, considering the circumstances.

Inspiration

The knowledge that conflicts contribute to the team building helps everyone concerned to keep their head in the heat of the moment. Executives should therefore be aware that, especially in heterogeneous teams, conflicts aren't only to be expected but also make sense. For the team too, this awareness can be helpful, particularly in the emotional *storming* phase.

When people get married, they are often reminded that

this is for good times and bad times, because a marriage is also an adventure in which you have to stick together. It's good to know beforehand that conflicts are part of it. It increases the chances toward a long and lively relationship when you don't simply separate after the first argument.

Functioning as a Team
— *Performing*

We didn't always live in harmony together, but we functioned. And we were a successful team, because we reached our overarching goal. All hostages survived the kidnapping, and one reason for that was that in crucial moments we always cooperated as a team.

In the day-to-day life in the jungle, we routinely helped each other and pooled communal tasks. We agreed on rules of behavior that would confirm our common survival strategy, and we coordinated our responses to the outside world so we wouldn't act against each other. Of course, those agreements weren't always kept, discussed, and actualized, but that was one of our fundamental strengths. Functioning teams and relationships aren't successful because they don't argue, but because they stay in contact and work for solutions "in good times as in bad times." In an extreme situation, it's generally easier to get over oneself and to help someone you have been angry with a short while before.

There were several suicide attempts in the hostage group. Some tried to kill themselves with an overdose of tranquilizers. Another person ran into the jungle with a knife to cut his wrists. But each time, one of the group recognized the danger and was able to prevent the worst. In one situation, I experienced the necessary cooperation for survival in two roles at once—as a helper and as the one being helped.

It was the fourteenth day of our captivity, and my mother's health had turned from bad to worse. Only four days previously, we had been shot at for the first time by the Philippine military and had to flee to another hideaway. It was incredibly hot, and we had hardly any water. On the long trek through the night, my mother collapsed and couldn't walk anymore. When we arrived in our open-air camp, she fell into a comatose sleep in her hammock. I was glad that she could sleep after all the hardship, but after a few hours began to worry whether she was unconscious and dehydrated, as she hadn't had any water for hours. I tried to wake her up and give her some water, but she was very dazed and too weak to sit up. I tried to pour some water into her mouth from the big gallon canister, but it went the wrong way down.

A short time later she said, "I don't want it anymore," and I thought that she didn't want more water, but she meant her life. She had given up, but I wasn't accepting that and became desperate. I felt immense relief shortly afterwards when a female doctor we had insisted on arrived.

But the relief didn't last, because she tried in vain to put an infusion cannula into my mother's arm and eventually said, "I have to leave the camp now, it's getting dark soon."

We were aghast, but she reassured us by saying that one of the rebels was capable of starting the infusion. And indeed, one of the rebels began wildly pricking a needle into the back of my mother's hand. She winced with pain and again swallowed the wrong way down and started fighting for air. During the whole time of our kidnapping and captivity, this was the worst moment and the only one in which I stopped functioning rationally. Helplessly, I ran in the direction of where the doctor had disappeared and shouted, "Get the fucking doctor back or we will carry my mother out of here!" I was determined to save my mother's life and to take any necessary risk.

Several rebels blocked my way and indicated with their weapons and handcuffs that they would rather kill me than let me go. I shouted at them in desperation and eventually did what they were asking me. I sat down, in the middle of the path—and cried. Several other hostages came and tried to placate the rebels. What touched me very much was that Stéphane, normally quite an aggressive man, talked to me in a calming way and told me that my mother was able again to breathe and swallow. While I was away, Marie had performed mouth-to-mouth resuscitation and prevented my mother from suffocating. Marie had surpassed herself, as, at that point, she wasn't actually fond of my mother.

In critical situations, the team always functioned well. As a group, we were more than the sum of our members. Time and again we cooperated, particularly when the situation was critical. The better our situation was, the more destructive the conflicts became. At the end of our captivity, our supply situation was much improved, we had enough to eat and things that made our life easier, but also more time to argue about trivial things, such as the fair sharing of muesli bars.

I have experienced similar conflict situations as an executive. Often it was about the equipment in the workplace. At a certain point, it's not about whether a larger computer screen makes sense for the tasks at hand, but that your colleague has one and you don't. It's about status and not about practicality. This is quite normal for humans, but poisonous for the atmosphere and the readiness of the team to cooperate. Sometimes less is indeed more. Never assume that better circumstances will automatically lead to a better group result.

We were a successful team, even though we hardly ever felt that way. Every team should celebrate its success from time to time—but celebrating was not on our agenda. We were too trapped by our fear of an uncertain future and stressed out by the daily challenges and conflicts; thus, we could never honor the battles we had won together.

To stop and celebrate is important—especially in times of great challenges and stress. What was hardly possible for us in the jungle, is often forgotten in the corporate world. As a consultant with PwC, I had a positive experience of this. For more than a year, our team of twenty consultants had been with a client at their place to manage an IT investment worth a billion euros. Stress was a constant issue as our client confronted us with ever-changing demands that we then had to try to meet during night shifts. The mood in the team shifted from panic to frustration because it felt that we were constantly extinguishing wildfires and didn't make any progress. The fluctuation within the team was high; we constantly had to replace team members who had quit with exhaustion. In the middle of it, our senior executive from Belgium announced his visit. We feared that he would put more pressure on us and would try to motivate us with encouraging phrases. But it turned out differently. All consultants were invited for half a day to the headquarters to hear an "important message."

The senior executive indeed had an important message for us. He succinctly described the situation we had to face day by day with the client and put it into perspective. "You are all in a very difficult phase of the project, with the most difficult client we have. You're doing a sensationally good job, and you have already done 70 percent of the work."

He then backed up everything he had said with data and facts. At the end of the meeting, we knew what we were fighting for, what milestones we had already reached, and when the battle would be over. It was extremely motivating that our work was recognized and acknowledged. But it was also reassuring that we had recognized our own performance, and it felt really, really good to celebrate our success.

Inspiration

If day-to-day business threatens to sink a team, or make it lose its head, only one thing can help: getting out of the melee, pausing, reassessing and celebrating whatever successes the team has had. If you find yourself responding to the panic by saying, "I don't have time for all this", you need to take some time out.

Welded Together in Need, but Not Forever — *Adjourning*

Many people assume that we hostages became a devoted community and that the members to this day are in touch. That's not the case, however—at least not for the whole group. Our time in the jungle had made us come closer than you probably ever get under normal circumstances, and maybe one wouldn't want that. But afterwards, each of us returned to their home and their previous life.

Contact between us has gotten less frequent in the last few years, and that's not even surprising, because apart from diving, we didn't have that much in common. The exceptional situation that bonded us together happened twenty years ago and ended, more or less, at the time of our release. Most of us were glad that they didn't have to adapt to the others anymore. Some of us didn't like each other very much, and that hasn't changed in freedom. After our release, some vented their anger at other members and so cleared the air for themselves as they processed their time in the jungle. Our Asian fellow sufferers were not interested in getting in touch with the Western hostages after our release, and I can understand that very well.

In some cases, however, real friendships formed on Jolo that last to this day. Callie and Monique had planned during their captivity to have children, and Marie later became godmother to their son. But no unswerving friendships have been formed, and so far, there have been no annual meetings or a party to celebrate our freedom.

Shortly after our release, I visited Marie in Paris and Callie and Monique in South Africa and have kept up occasional email contact with them ever since. Last year, I visited my Finnish fellow sufferers in Helsinki to find out how they had done since our release. It was a lovely reunion after nineteen years, and also quite telling. Again, I realized that we all dealt with the experience differently, with some quite exotic examples. Seppo, for example, had, during our captivity, expressed his feelings in drawings. After our release, he concentrated on the topic of how fear is expressed in art and he is now an expert and collector of contemporary art in Finland.

The dissolution of a team is the fifth and last phase during team building and it is important to utilize the results in a sustainable way. During the hectic day-to-day life, this phase is often cut short.

It makes sense, however, to ask project teams to document the results of their work before they get lost in their everyday work. I remember a certain moment back in Luxembourg when I sat with four other consultants in the office at night to finish a one hundred fifty-page report for our client. At three in the morning it was completed, and the project manager said, "Okay, the first monthly report for the board has been finished after two months of hard work. Congratulations! Thank you! But before you go to your well-deserved rest, please create an online file with all the data!" I was speechless. "What?" That will be another hour! It's three in the morning! Can't we do it tomorrow?"

He answered firmly, "No. We'll avoid that mistake. Tomorrow it's back to daily routines, and for the next monthly report we would have to start again from scratch. It would mean chaos, stress, and night shifts again." It was a hard but good lesson in terms of "finishing a project and documentation."

During the last weeks of our captivity, we did with dedication what in the day-to-day hubbub of a business is often neglected. We documented our experiences with cameras and diaries. Admittedly, we had much more time, and it was good to look forward to and think of the time after our release, which was happening in stages. After the first hostages were released, freedom appeared to be within reach; the end of our time together was conceivable. We exchanged our contact details, and took some goodbye photos of the ones who were left. The order in which we were set free was more or less accepted, with some exceptions, and we were always happy for the ones who could leave the camp to freedom.

Most of the Western hostages kept a diary during their captivity and published it as a book after their release. The titles were *Horror in a Tropical Paradise,* by Werner Wallert, my father; *Shooting the Moon,* by Callie and Monique Strydom; *Jolo* by Seppo Franti and Risto Vahanen; *Otage à Jolo* (*Hostages on Jolo*) by Stéphane Loisy; and *Mon père m'attandait a Manille* (*My Father Waited for Me in Manila*) by Marie Moarbes.

It's very interesting how differently we all experienced and processed the time on Jolo. The chronological data and facts match, but the evaluation of other captives and situations vary a lot and mirror the character of the observer, the author—frustrated, conciliatory, reflective, impulsive, rational, and spiritual.

I wrote down my observations during my captivity with the meticulousness of an ethnologist, on hundreds of pages, not with a view to later publish it, but to be able to remember everything. Once, for example, I filled more than twenty pages describing every step and every moment of a single day to be able to recollect later how we had felt and behaved in our daily life on Jolo.

Today, twenty years later, I realize how valuable these records are and can see them in a wider context. Emotionally I feel detached now and understand why I survived the kidnapping so well. In my private as well as in my working life, time and again I recognize parallels to the jungle experience, and so I could benefit from my time on Jolo. Now the time has come to share those experiences with other people.

Inspiration

In or immediately after a difficult time or project, we often lack the strength and the time to document it. But this is worthwhile, because memories fade, connections get simplified or even twisted, and important insights for the future get lost. It's very helpful, especially in turbulent periods, to document everything, either in a private diary or in a project file.

Success Factors of an Agile Team

Time and again, I've asked myself how such a motley crew managed under such adverse conditions to cooperate so well and so successfully. As I have described, there were conflicts, but they were part of the process and an important step in the team-building process. Apart from that, there were other factors that significantly contributed to our success. I read about some of these factors later in an article entitled "Agile Teams in the VUCA World." Agile? VUCA? I didn't know those terms. But the content was surprisingly familiar, because it corresponded to our situation then and how we dealt with it. Uncertain, complex, and fast-moving times challenge us to respond in an agile and flexible way. Particularly suited for that are decentralized, autonomous, and interdisciplinary teams. This is a summary of a concept that in the last few years has been bandied about in management literature under the terms of *Agility* and *VUCA*. For me, those terms express our jungle experiences as well as the success factors of our team. Because at work, time and again, I noticed that the principles for successful work, whether in the jungle or in the corporate world, are very similar.

The VUCA World —
an Obscure Jungle of Changes

VUCA is an acronym for the terms *volatility, uncertainty, complexity,* and *ambiguity.* It describes characteristics of our changing world, marked by ever faster and more complex changes, such as digitalization and globalization. People as well as organizations are faced with big challenges, as the future is getting more unpredictable and making long-term decisions and plans is becoming increasingly difficult.

For companies, the VUCA world means that traditional leadership and organizational principles don't fit anymore. As a specialist in organizational control, I have experienced this firsthand. In 2011, I was responsible for a five-year plan for a market leader in medical technology. Together with four other team members, I coordinated the cost and turnover planning for more than one hundred departments in fifty countries, which were to be distilled into concrete action plans. Accounts, personnel, product development, marketing, and distribution were dependent on each other and had to be coordinated and consolidated for each country, each region, and globally.

This mammoth task lasted for more than six months and didn't only drive me and my team mad, but the whole international management team to its limits. Typical irritated comments included: "Why not use a crystal ball?" "How do I know what turnover of which products I will make in five years?" and "We really need totally different products for our local market than you produce in your headquarters, and we need them now!"

In their need, most of the people responsible for the planning limited themselves to projecting past developments into the future. That exact tactic, however, is a mistake. In a faster-moving world of changes, the predictability of future events on the basis of previous experience is as reliable as a five-year weather forecast. Stock markets crash, disturbing technologies revolutionize the markets, and the time span for developing new products gets ever shorter.

Hierarchical structures in organizations and leadership principles are too cumbersome to respond quickly to changes in external conditions. Organizations, more and more, make use of agile, decentralized teams that are able to respond autonomously and more quickly to external changes. Surprisingly, the trailblazer in this is the military, which is hierarchical and follows a strict top-down principle of command and control. But small, ready-to-act combat troops ("squads") typically consisting of nine soldiers are the predecessors of agile teams. And they were an answer to changes in many other external conditions as well.

The term VUCA originated in the 1990s at the U.S. Army War College as a reaction to the end of the Cold War and to the bitter experiences of guerrilla wars such as in Vietnam. Modern warfare has only very little to do with the historical battles in which large armies of two countries faced each other. In times of terrorism, the boundaries between war and peace, front and hinterland, enemy and civilian, are fluid. As hostages, we experienced this firsthand in the middle of a guerrilla war.

For us, our kidnappers were a motley bunch of fighters and farmers. Sometimes we asked ourselves ironically whether we were victims of organized or disorganized crime, without really knowing which we would have preferred. It was exactly this unpredictability that made our kidnappers invincible. We frequently moved from one hideout to another. The hostage group was repeatedly broken up for tactical reasons, in case the military attacked. We never found out which of the five rebel leaders was actually the boss. We couldn't even clearly decide who among our kidnappers was a rebel, a civilian, a policeman, or a soldier. Some of the kidnappers had been in the Philippine military until recently and simply wore their army T-shirts. Others put down their weapons temporarily and then couldn't be distinguished from a simple farmer. There were children, about twelve years old, holding machine guns, with munition belts slung over their shoulders. At that point, the identities of our enemies became completely blurred.

I can't precisely say how the rebels' guerrilla tactics worked, but the military could not defeat them. The three thousand soldiers the Philippine army deployed didn't achieve anything during our kidnapping, apart from randomly shooting at us at times. Nor did they succeed after our release to "wipe out" the rebel group Abu Sayyaf for good, as then-Philippine president Joseph Estrada repeatedly promised—not even with the support of the American military.

Let's consider the set of VUCA challenges that our team faced in the jungle:

V is for "volatile" — That applied to everything around us. The weather changed frequently, and we even experienced a typhoon. The mood of the kidnappers could also change rapidly. Minor quarrels between the rebels could easily escalate into a fight or gunfire in the middle of our camp.

U is for "uncertainty" — For us, this primarily meant that at no time did we have any idea whether or when we would be released. Any predictions about our release were pure speculation. We couldn't even guess whether we would be staying in the same camp for another day or would suddenly have to flee again.

C is for "complex" — This describes the whole situation. Our fate depended on a number of factors, which in turn were dependent on one other. The negotiations about our release were influenced by constantly changing chief negotiators, embassies of seven governments, the vague leadership structure of the rebels, reports by international media, and our health.

A is for "ambiguous" — Our relationship to the various parties was always ambiguous. Was our bodyguard our protector or our mortal enemy? Was the Philippine army our potential liberator or a threat to our lives? Did the people from the local villages delivering our food support us or were they sympathetic to the rebels? Were the journalists helping us to communicate, or were they only there for their own benefit and profit? And how was I to judge Islamist freedom fighters who gave themselves names like "Rambo" or "Van Damme" and called me "hero" or "idol"?

The situation wasn't easy, the boundaries fluid, the future uncertain, and the mixture of factors obscure. Only one thing was clear: we couldn't behave the way we were accustomed to or would have liked to. Planning and control were not possible. Instead, we had to react in an agile and flexible way to the events in our VUCA world. Luckily, we managed most of the time.

We Were an Agile Team

Our involuntary group experiment was unique and, in that sense, differed from normal life. In an organization, you can establish an agile team and methods, but we couldn't introduce processes, structures, or procedures, and there was no kick-off workshop either. The VUCA-like conditions didn't develop over time but became our reality from day one.

This radical change wasn't a disadvantage in every sense.

It meant, for instance, that we were forced to adapt our behavior immediately. For this reason, the following illustrations are not meant to be a blueprint for the introduction of agile principles in a modern organization. Not all of our jungle strategies can be transferred to a business context. But as an executive, I found out how useful my experiences in the jungle could be for coping with VUCA challenges in an organization.

One Common Vision: Survival!

If your life is in immediate danger, apart from fear, something very valuable emerges: clarity. Everyday problems fade into the background and leave only one goal—survival. While I was still on the kidnappers' boat, I realized that this adventure was entirely about survival, and it felt as if a burden was taken off my shoulders. All the worries about my job and my relationships were suddenly unimportant. I didn't have to make any decisions about what career path I wanted to take or how to manage my love life. Survival was the only priority. That's how I learned that sometimes difficult times make decision-making much easier.

As we hostages all sat in one boat, each of us had the same goal—we wanted to survive. And we wanted to do it all together. Was our mutual support an act of human kindness? Yes, partly. But there was another, equally important motive, which didn't have much to do with altruism. We were all afraid that one of us might die, and that would have made it clear to us how much danger we were all in. It would have dashed our hopes for our own survival. The confidence of the group would have dropped to zero.

From the beginning, we were unified by one vision—all of us surviving. I remember the moment when we were discussing a possible escape. We quickly agreed that a single person fleeing was not an option because the lives of the remaining hostages would then be at a massive risk. It was also absurd to believe that a group of twenty-one could escape from the jungle without anyone noticing. Therefore, we concentrated on remaining fit physically and mentally until we were released.

Such a strong and clear common vision was definitely one of the most significant drivers toward success. There were no profound discussions about what it meant. The central goal was clear and didn't have to be developed in lengthy group discussions. We all had the same image in our head and could concentrate on realizing it—survival! To achieve the goal, we had to do two things: we would try to push for our release as soon as possible, and we would see to it that we stayed alive until that day. Every one of us contributed toward the common goal.

In comparison with modern organizations, our hostage group had a crucial advantage—a common vision. No one had to be motivated or convinced. The reality in most teams and companies is different. The alignment of all members to a common goal is much more complex.

In my seventeen years in the corporate world, I created and experienced some more-or-less successful methods for this, including employee surveys, workshops, and communication events to create a common ground. It generally ended with the publication of a pamphlet called "Vision Paper," "Mission Statement," or "Company Philosophy." Unfortunately, the process typically ended there, even though it was meant to be only the starting point for the day-to-day application of the agreed fundamentals.

However, people usually only change their behavior when they have no other choice. A tangible crisis, like a dramatic drop in sales, can actually help to initiate and implement difficult changes. The best solution, however, is to anticipate crises, to prepare employees during the good times for future risks, and to motivate them for innovative changes.

In families too, the orientation toward a common life plan needs repeated discussions and adaptation. Often it is about issues such as save or spend, travel or get settled, move house or stay—in other words freedom or safety. Ironically, freedom and safety were not contradictory notions in our situation, but mutually dependent ones. A common vision is particularly important for so-called agile organizations, because the single members and teams act flexibly and autonomously. The alignment of all activities and priorities toward a common goal is fundamentally important.

Inspiration

Teams need a common vision, particularly when they must act quickly and independently from others. Ask your employees or colleagues whether they have a clear vision. If they say yes, ask them whether they all have the same vision or whether each person has a separate one.

No Boss

As hostages, we were always at the mercy of our kidnappers. They took power over us with violence and could decide over our life or death with their weapons. At first, this came as a shock, because we were all used to planning our lives ourselves. Initially, we tried to speculate about a possible release date and discussed it, trying to gain a tiny bit of control over our fate. But we had no way of predicting the time of our release. Amazingly, we were given a lot of leeway to help us adapt to our situation. For example, we were allowed to organize our food supply independently and did not need to rely on the rebels for this.

Did we get organized as a group to make the best of our situation? A common question is, "Did you have a kind of leader?" Until my captivity, I had been convinced that groups always had a leader. My assumption was advanced by the novel *Lord of the Flies* by William Golding. It describes the social development of a group of children who find themselves on an uninhabited tropical island. In the end, two groups with one leader each fight each other to the death.

A Network with Clear Roles

It is interesting that there was no leader in our group—neither in a formal nor an informal capacity. There was no power struggle either in the sense of "I'm the boss here" "No, I am!" like there is in so many groups where there is always someone who needs to make his mark. Maybe we guessed that in our situation this wouldn't make sense. In fact, there was a kind of leadership, but it fluctuated, depending on what challenges were imminent. In the first few days, my father spoke for the group because of his fluent English and, as the oldest person, he enjoyed some respect from the rebels.

When we were talking about practical things, we always looked up to Stéphane, who was an engineer. With his sense for practicalities (I called it *savoir survivre*) he sometimes led a team, for example when building a roof of bamboo and plastic sheets as a shelter from the rain. In medical emergencies, Marie was called for as a paramedic and Seppo as a nurse. They also took responsibility for keeping and distributing our medicines. In addition to being a general helper, every now and then I was approached to take on the role of mediator. In arguments between my parents and the French hostages, my knowledge of the language and my diplomatic and moderating skills were helpful. Aida was the interpreter between us and the Filipinos, particularly in language and cultural issues, even though she plainly disliked the role. Callie led the prayer circle and was something of a moral and spiritual leader. Risto didn't communicate very much, but when he said something in his calm way, it was to the point. He was the first to call for a meeting about group conflicts and he then chaired it. His experience as a business leader was noticeable, and Commander Robot, one of the rebel leaders, is said to have washed Risto's feet once after a long night trek—a sign of ultimate respect. But even Risto wasn't our chosen or named leader.

We didn't have a boss, no ultimate top dog who made the final decisions. And that was a good thing, because a hierarchical structure wouldn't have helped us in the jungle. The VUCA situation was much too unpredictable for that. What was needed was flexibility and speed. If all decisions had to be confirmed by a leader—or worse, by someone outside the jungle—we would have been far too slow, when, for example, we had to quickly erect a shelter from the approaching rain and cut up two sleeping bags for that purpose. We could make decisions autonomously and apply the necessary skills as and when required.

Diversity

The different characters and competencies within the group were a blessing and a curse at the same time. On the one hand, diversity is a great asset, especially when one has to respond to any number of rapid changes autonomously and in a decentralized way. For that, you need an interdisciplinary team representing all the relevant skills to master complex challenges. On the other hand, in a heterogenous group like that, there are necessarily more conflicts and misunderstandings than in a homogenous group that (literally) speaks the same language.

But no group of people is ever truly homogenous. Whenever ten people come together, they won't all be leaders or optimists. At least, they won't stay that way. As soon as the group has formed, other important roles are taken on. For example, people become supporters and critics. It's not a question of whether those roles are taken on, but rather of who takes them on.

In our case, roles went to the weak members. My mother and Seppo, as previously mentioned, took them on, at least for a time. This admittedly unenviable role was valuable for the group for two reasons. We could use my mother's ill health to put pressure on the negotiations. We could credibly state that our quick release wouldn't be simply "nice," but essential. This helped our communications with the outside world. But there was also a positive side effect within the group. I was allocated the role of helper, which was very comfortable. Others in the group could regard themselves as stronger because some members had taken on the weaker roles.

Stay Flexible

The reality of most organizations and teams is different, however. Clients asking for help often get the response, "That's not my department" or "I have to ask the boss first." But we didn't have time for such tactics. We had to act and cooperate. And that's what we did, for example, when I flipped out after my mother collapsed. I changed roles with Stéphane, and he turned into a diplomat and intervened to placate the situation. He didn't only calm me down, but the kidnappers also.

The flexibility of roles is not only a great advantage in a group, but also in a relationship. Maybe this sounds familiar to you: one partner is rather an optimist, the other more of a pessimist or realist. Both roles are important, the dreaming and the assessing of risks. When the roles get reversed and the optimist has a bad day and the pessimist encourages him or her, the team functions well.

Inspiration

Agile teams have the advantage of being able to respond quickly and flexibly to a dynamic situation. Sometimes, it is a necessary and rational reaction to the challenges of the VUCA world, but it doesn't mean that working in an agile way is necessarily easy or fun. Conflicts within interdisciplinary teams are preprogrammed, as all joint actions have to be agreed with one other. It's important that team members know their professional and informal roles and that the conflicts get resolved constructively.

Finding Solutions Through Constant Communication

Transparency is one of the elemental principles of agile teams. For that purpose, all members meet once a day for a short stand-up meeting to inform each other of the latest developments and to discuss possible changes of action. There is no fixed plan that has to be worked through step by step, and there is no boss to coordinate the activities of the members. Therefore, constant communication among team members is vital for success.

In our case, the communication developed spontaneously, because we lived in close proximity in our jungle camp, seven days a week, twenty-four hours a day. We did get on each other's nerves, but the closeness also had vital advantages in our situation. We quickly learned from each other and copied survival strategies from each other. In the corporate world, you would call that best-practice sharing. For example, one of the rebels had shown Marie how to turn a rice sack into a backpack. You cut long strips of fiber from the soft bark of a banana tree and knot them as straps to the two corners of the rice sack. The sack is open at the top but can be closed with another strip of fiber. Done. This invention was invaluable. We could transport our few belongings much more easily when we had to change camp. It kept our hands free, to either find our way through a thicket or to carry additional water containers.

News also traveled quickly around our constricted living arrangements and made it possible for us to respond quickly to critical changes. When one of us was able to organize a new channel of communication or a new food delivery, we heard about it immediately and all benefited from it. When one of us got medicine from his embassy, we could make sure it would go to the person who at that moment was most in need of it.

When Marie was asked by one of the rebels whether she had medicine for tuberculosis, we knew that we had to work on our hygiene standards even more. When the news of a helicopter waiting in the island's capital blared out from one of the transistor radios, we could prepare for my mother's release—thanks to Aida's translation. This and many more examples show how constructive a quick flow of information can be.

Most of all—and most quickly—we learned from our mistakes. If we failed badly, we were prepared the next time. When we had to flee from an army attack for the first time, we ran out of the camp in panic and left most of our important gadgets and our small amount of water behind. The trek became much more arduous because of this.

We were better prepared the second time. We each had an escape rucksack ready and had seen to it that there was always an extra gallon of fresh water within easy reach. With each experience, we adapted better to the dynamic challenges. In business, you call it "iterative project management."

When we had to flee for a second time, my mother was not able to walk, as she was dehydrated and partially unconscious. My father and I decided to carry her out of the camp, if needed. Callie and Stéphane suggested that we make a stretcher of two long branches and a plastic sheet, which we could carry on our shoulders. We completed it after a few attempts. Without this stretcher, we could never have taken my mother on our second escape from the military. The stretcher, in the end, had to last a whole day and a night until we reached the next camp. I can't imagine what would have happened if we hadn't all cooperated so closely.

Thanks to our constant communication, our learning curve in intercultural things was also steep. In the beginning, we believed everything our captors said. When many of them suddenly started to take their hammocks and tents down, we asked for the reason and they told us, "No panic, just relax!" When we asked whether we needed to prepare for another trek, they generally answered, "No, we stay here." A minute later it was, "Move, move, move." Then we frantically needed to leave the camp. Aida explained that the rebels, even when they knew what was happening, wouldn't give the honest answer, but a "friendly" one. It was part of their culture and not meant to be a damaging lie. Thanks to Aida, we were able to solve this misunderstanding fairly quickly and didn't get angry about the lies anymore. Instead we followed Aida's advice: "Be ready, at any time."

Learning from Mistakes

We were alarmed when we first heard a strange sound in the distance and the rebels suddenly ran around wildly shouting, "Ulan! Ulan!" Then we were surprised by a massive downpour of rain and learned that "Ulan" in the local language Tagalog means "hard rain."

We learned quickly, from each other and from our mistakes, because we could see clearly that what had happened once could happen again and could possibly cost us our lives. None of us felt we had to prove anything, and there was no shame in admitting to mistakes. It meant that we were highly solution-focused, because, after all, this was about our survival.

In the corporate world, you can't take it for granted that people will learn from their mistakes. Most companies boast of a "culture of mistakes," but the reality is different. Mistakes are considered a failure and get quickly and shamefully hidden or blamed on others. Customer complaints are frequently put into a different context instead of explored. Drops in turnover are glossed over instead of the reasons investigated. This is not surprising because managers would rather punish their employees instead of respecting their honesty.

As an executive, I have experienced how difficult it is to establish a culture of openly admitting mistakes. I looked into many puzzled faces when, at the end of a meeting, I gave the following advice to a team: "After the event, please try to get hold of as much critical feedback as you can."

Before then, it was normal in training to measure clients' satisfaction with feedback documents called "happy sheets." The trainers were glad when most of the participants put crosses on the left side, meaning "very good" and, even better, added a positive comment. And now the boss was asking to collect negative feedback? Yes, because he knew before the pilot project that we would be making mistakes and the expectations of the participants wouldn't always be met. But we didn't know exactly what those mistakes would be. If we planned to introduce the new format as standard and offer it on a regular basis, we had to learn from this pilot project and from future events to continually learn and improve our input. The last and most important milestone in a project plan is called "lessons learned" for precisely that reason.

Changes take time. After four years, I was invited to a lessons-learned meeting, but not to moderate it. It gave me great pleasure to see how matter-of-fact the six participants were as they sat together and rationally discussed critical comments and potential for improvement.

Due to our involuntary closeness and constant communication in the jungle, we could avoid the kind of misunderstandings and delays that in day-to-day work can arise when using phones or emails. We could instead develop close cooperation. But as soon as we were split up into smaller groups, the synergy dropped. There were hardly any exchanges between the Western and the Asian groups, even though we were only a short distance apart. Once, when our Western group was split up between two bamboo platforms, the cooperation was immediately more difficult. Close proximity automatically creates team spirit, and random, unplanned synergies develop.

It's no different on a normal day in the office. Open offices and flexi desks are an attempt to enhance communication within a department or across several departments. This is not very popular, because most people prefer their own space in which to work, surrounded by their colleagues.

Inspiration

Speed and adaptability of teams and organizations have become significant factors for success in the era of VUCA.

What helps is an appropriate culture of learning, enabling direct communication. It also helps to use mistakes constructively rather than punishing people or teams that make them.

Positive Thinking Can Be Deadly — in Business Too

Optimism Is a Double-Edged Sword

Without a doubt, optimism helped the other hostages and me cope with the difficult time in the jungle. The firm belief that at some point we would enjoy life in freedom again gave us strength. And the clearer this vision was, the greater was our hope. But we have to be careful with optimism in uncertain times! It is a double-edged sword. The belief in a positive ending gives us strength, but the belief in a quick ending can weaken the stamina for endurance. The optimists among us predicted a swift release and paid for it with great disappointment and emotional lows. It gets even more dangerous when positive thinking dulls your view of reality. If you underestimate a danger, you're not well equipped for risky situations to come.

Positive thinking is generally something to appreciate and it is an important factor for success. The same applies to the corporate world, but it's bad when companies in their endless optimism ignore real risks. This is especially true in times of disruption and digitalization. Some companies came to bitterly regret their beliefs (or hopes) such as:

"Digitalization? That's just a trend that will quickly disappear!" or "Our products and processes are long tested and successful—we'll simply carry on as before."

Some companies can even go bankrupt because of their positive thinking. Market leaders are at particular peril because quite often they tend to project their past success into the future. They trust the enduring triumph of their proven products and rest on the laurels of their success as market leaders. They don't recognize the risks arising from innovative technologies or business models. Nokia and Kodak lost their heads in a cloud of optimism. Nokia considered itself to be so well set up with its famous cellphone that it dramatically underestimated the future of the smartphone. In 2013, Nokia paid for the mistake with the loss of its cellphone branch. Kodak had to file for bankruptcy in 2012 because the company had underestimated the tremendous success of digital photography. This was particularly tragic, as Kodak had developed a prototype of a digital camera in-house. But the company was too optimistic that its normal, successful analog cameras would be good enough for the future. It was a fatal error.

Today, I consider one of my most important jungle experiences to be that I kept my head emotionally. I was neither paralyzed by fear of death, nor did I relax prematurely, assuming we would be released quickly. It helped me to believe in a positive ending, but at the same time I prepared in a realistic way for a long and difficult time in the jungle. This split between optimism and realism isn't easy—but it's optimal in uncertain times. The attitude is also a central factor for success in the corporate world. This is scientifically proven.

The Right Attitude for Success in Business

Jim Collins, an management expert, describes seven management principles for enduring success in business in his global bestseller *Good to Great*. One of them is "Confront the brutal facts (Yet never lose faith)". Top companies are characterized by the fact that they avoid the kind of mistakes Nokia and Kodak made by effectively dealing with risks and crises in the market. Collins explores how top companies behave in a crisis and states that in all cases the management responds to the challenges with an effective psychological two-way approach. On the one hand, they acknowledge the hard facts with stoic calmness, while at the same time they believe in a positive outcome.

Collins calls this two-way approach the "Stockdale Paradox," named after Jim Stockdale. From 1965–1973, Stockdale was the highest-ranking American officer in the Vietnamese prisoner of war camp known as the Hanoi Hilton, where he was tortured more than twenty times. After his release, he was promoted to vice admiral in the U.S. Navy. While in captivity, Stockdale's survival strategy was to keep believing that one will prevail in the end, no matter how difficult it will be, but at the same time must face the brutal facts of the current situation, no matter how unpleasant they are. Not all prisoners of war survived their ordeal in Vietnam. When asked "Who didn't make it?" Stockdale answered, "The optimists. They were the ones who said, 'We're going to be out by Christmas.' And Christmas would come, and Christmas would go. Then they'd say, 'We're going to be out by Easter.' And Easter would come, and Easter would go. And then Thanksgiving, and then it would be Christmas again. And they died of a broken heart."

To be robust and successful, companies need to walk the line between optimism and realism in the same way that helped Jim Stockdale in Hanoi and me on Jolo. But how does this work in the corporate world? It's not a trivial matter, as I have experienced myself in my career.

The Arrival of Digitalization

Sooner or later, digitalization will be knocking at the door of every company. It offers great opportunities but also includes risks. That's why not everyone embraces it. Quite the opposite. The first responses to the digital transformation were a mixture of ignoring it, mocking it, and cursing it.

When I was a project manager with Renault, I was involved in the introduction and digital transformation of the ordering and logistics systems in the car industry. For decades, the garages ordered spare parts by phone or fax. Now they were to use a more efficient online ordering system. When the changes were announced, the employees in the garages reacted by rolling their eyes rather than clapping their hands.

This didn't improve when the new system was finally implemented. Users reacted with either skepticism or outright irritation when the online system wasn't working properly or when it crashed. But after the I.T. teething problems were dealt with, no one could even imagine returning to the old phone and fax system. After gaining this experience of a successful digital transformation, I later switched to the medical technological company Ottobock Healthcare. Ottobock had been a market leader for more than one hundred years producing prostheses and components in more than one hundred locations. It is the largest international supplier of prostheses. For five years beginning in 2013, I ran the competence center at the headquarters and was responsible for sixty employees in three locations at which patients were supplied with state-of-the-art leg prostheses and technicians were trained in orthopedics.

From behind the scenes, I watched the production of these high-tech prostheses with amazement. Traditionally, making prostheses is a craft, and the work mainly takes place in a workshop. One of the main components in many of the production stages is plaster, which needs to be kneaded, trimmed, and filed over and over again. These processes had existed for decades until digital alternatives were developed. Suddenly, the traditional craft was threatened by scanners, computer numerical control (CNC) milling, and 3D-printers. There were YouTube videos, in which small tech start-ups demonstrated how they could produce parts of a prothesis without any plaster, seemingly at the drop of a hat. The images looked as though they were from a sci-fi film, but they were doubtlessly appealing—not the least to the clients.

Luckily, Ottobock's then-CEO recognized the opportunity and didn't fall victim to false optimism. He not only took the challenge from innovative start-ups seriously, but also tried to learn from their example. Enthusiastically, he approached digital start-ups outside his field to explore the potential of the new technologies. He was an optimist, but of the kind who wouldn't rest on the laurels of the past. His clear vision was, "The workshop of the future is digital, with no plaster, and it is client-friendly." As a consequence, various departments of the company started to experiment and work with digital technology.

In my department, however, the skeptics retained the upper hand. Most of the specialists in my team didn't regard the new technologies as serious competitors to the time-honored production methods. Typical comments included, "Every handmade prosthesis fits 100 percent and lasts longer than the digital stuff"; or "No workshop without plaster—it's no place for clients"; or "An experienced craftsman cannot be replaced by a machine." I considered those statements to be true for the present time, but was reminded of Renault. The teething troubles of digital technologies would soon be resolved, and we certainly wanted to be at the cutting edge in our field. I decided to encourage my team and to whip up some enthusiasm for the opportunities of digitalization. But I fell into the optimism trap without knowing it.

Leading a Team Through Times of Uncertainty

The monthly meeting of the department was the first opportunity to convince my team of our CEO's vision. I had prepared three PowerPoint slides. The first one showed our CEO with his vision: "The workshop of the future is digital, plaster-free, and client-friendly." The reactions were rather restrained.

The second slide showed the orthopedics workshop—plaster everywhere. Headline: "A workshop without plaster? Really?" I said, "I understand that you cannot imagine a workshop without plaster. But the digitalization of orthopedic technology is only a question of time. At some point in the near future, you will not be able to even imagine working like you do today. I'm convinced of that because I have experienced this transition in the car industry already." Some of the employees shifted in their seats.

A third slide showed a garage with oil-covered tools and people in overalls and a modern, clean, light workshop with service personnel talking to clients. The headline ran, "A workshop without oil? Yes, it works!" I added, "Your plaster is like oil in the car industry. They believed too that oil was an essential part of a garage and that a garage was no place for customers. But when we go to a garage today, no mechanic approaches us with an oil-covered spanner in his hand. Instead, a mechatronic switch on a laptop diagnoses the car's problems digitally. The world of car servicing is already digital, clean, and customer friendly. Isn't that a great example?" But my enthusiasm wasn't really catching on. Instead, I detected irritation and resentment. What was happening?

An experienced member of the team explained it to me. He had been an orthopedic technician for forty-five years. With grudging respect, but helpfully, he gave me my lesson: "The people feel rejected when you, as their manager, tell them that you could turn everything digital in an instant. It's not that simple. You are much too optimistic. Apart from that, not everything is as bad as you have described. You should listen more to the experts."

His words shocked me because appreciation was so important to me. I hadn't meant to discourage or even snub anyone. A short time later, he had an idea which, in the end, led to success and initiated our digital transformation. "Why don't we analyze the last forty-five years of our competence center and look at all that we have achieved?

I can find some photos and videos from the archive. What do you think?" I agreed.

On a cold January morning at the beginning of a new year, the team gathered in a place that couldn't have been chosen more effectively as a location for launching the new strategic direction. It was the futuristic extension of the historic ancestral home of the company's owner. Here, the beginnings and the future of the family and the company were architecturally united.

The experienced orthopedic technician began by talking about the traditions of the company. He listed the technological achievements as well as the emotional highlights of the past few decades, illustrated by photos, videos, and anecdotes. His colleagues weren't only well entertained but also honored for their achievements. They were proud to have been part of it.

But then the presentation shifted to focusing on how to continue the success story and to lift the quality of patient care to new heights using revolutionary technologies. I added, "Some of the current digital solutions are not yet of the quality we demand. We need your skills to change this. We have a chance to be at the forefront of revolutionary technology development and to remain at the cutting edge of the industry. It won't be easy, but you have already demonstrated that it's possible by being the cutting edge of technical orthopedics up to now."

This time, I seemed to have found the right tone of voice. I sensed an increasing openness among the employees and a serious interest in the digital innovations. More and more, and with growing enthusiasm, they engaged in the pilot projects with scanners and 3D technology. In training, we also offered online courses, in addition to the traditional methods. Digital transformation had arrived to the team and our employees' satisfaction increased, despite the demanding changes.

Many executives in times of change make the same mistake that I made. They burst with optimism in the hope of giving their employees courage for impending changes. But you cannot quell fears and resistance with optimism. Many concerns are justified, not the least of which are fears over job security. A threat like "If you don't move with the times, you will be out sooner or later" doesn't work either. In communication, its necessary to strike a balance between realism ("the situation is serious"), optimism ("we will make it"), and the acknowledgment of fears ("I understand your concerns"). Only then will people who are fearful turn into people who are cooperative, and who can be won over to face imminent challenges.

Inspiration

In times of disruption and digitalization, it's important to keep one's head! But this can't be out of sheer optimism. The two most frequent and momentous errors of optimists are "Changes are not necessary" and "Changes are easy."

It is much more about recognizing the need for changes and addressing the imminent process of change with the necessary respect. During this phase, one should keep one eye on a good outcome and the other on the risks. The best attitude in times of uncertainty is a split between optimism and realism. It's not easy, but it works.

OUTLOOK

It is a good idea to accept changes as part of life and a chance for one's own progression. Life is full of transitions from one developmental step to the next. Admittedly, not all tests in life reveal their deeper meaning as clearly as some steps in human development, such as puberty. Events like a serious illness or sudden job loss are painful and we would love to keep them out of our lives. But those experiences are also part of life. Often, times of need lead us to turn our lives around for the better.

We cannot keep external stress out of our life altogether. But we can decide how we deal with it. Most of all, we can learn from it how to deal better with negative events in the future. In this sense, I would like to make a few suggestions of how you can enhance your inner strength and mental stamina.

These six protective factors of resilience helped me to get through the kidnapping with strength: acceptance, optimism, stress management, self-efficacy, social support, and fitness and discipline. I'd like to invite you—through some questions and suggestions—to bring those protective factors into your everyday life. You decide which of the inspirations are useful and actionable for you.

Acceptance: How to meet a challenge without battling against fate.

As long as we struggle with our fate, our energy is focused on the past and will be found lacking when dealing with current challenges. As soon as possible after a negative event, it's important to accept that a situation has changed and to make the most of it. The following can help:

- Ask yourself: Is there an event in your life you struggle with? Are your thoughts focused on questions like "Why me?" or statements like "I wish I had …" or "If only that hadn't happened"?
- Write down your thoughts, maybe in a diary. This alone can have a liberating effect as you change from ruminating to being active. Also, you can deal with your thoughts better when you look at them with some detachment.
- Ask yourself whether that was the worst that could have happened. You might find it easier to accept your situation.
- Grief counselling. Everyone grieves in their own way and in their own time. But if you have lost a loved one, professional help can support you in dealing with the loss.
- With many serious events, it's helpful to be clear

that what has happened has happened. You can't turn the clock back.

- To accept a negative event, it might help to think, "Maybe it was for the best." Can you make sense of the event? Can you draw any positives from your new situation?
- Don't blame yourself if you cannot accept your situation. Accept that you cannot accept the situation and at least make peace with yourself.

Optimism: How to cope with difficult times with a positive attitude and with the power of visualization.

Optimism can help you overcome blows more quickly and more easily. It is also proven to have a positive effect on your physical and mental health. A positive attitude attracts other people and supplies you with a social network that might support you. Here are some suggestions of how you can adjust your attitude during difficult times from the negative "I'll never cope with that!" to a more positive "I'm gonna make it!"

- In times of stress, use the power of imagination to gain strength and confidence. Use all your senses to imagine a positive image of your future. What does it look like? How does it feel? What can I hear? What does it smell like? Successful athletes use this technique to remain positive during the stress of a competition.

- Focus on positive things. In the morning, right after waking up, imagine three things you can look forward to that day. In the evening, give thanks for three things for which you can be grateful. It could be little things, such as the sun shining that day.
- Surround yourself with optimists. You can learn how to adopt a positive attitude from role models around you. Avoid pessimists who repeatedly turn your thoughts into negatives.
- Smile, even if there is nothing to smile about. If necessary, put a pen between your lips for a minute, as long as the corners of your mouth turn upwards. Emotions not only show on our features, it also works the other way around. The way we look has an impact on our feelings.
- If you feel overburdened, take small steps forward and praise yourself for your successes. It's a way to increase your confidence to eventually get a grip on a situation.

Stress management skills: How to keep your head in a crisis.

Have you had situations in your life when something existential is under threat, such as your health, your relationship, or your income? A critical illness, a relationship crisis, or a phase of unemployment can last for a long time and demands increased attention and actions to turn it around to something positive. In phases like that, being stressed makes sense to a certain degree. It propels us into action and averts dangers. But stress turns into a problem when it lasts for a long time and cannot be relieved by periods of relaxation. At work, stress threatens the well-being of people more and more. According to a study on stress by a German insurer, there has been an increase in sickness through stress over the past fifteen years. A typical person has fifteen days off per year, two-and-a-half of which they take due to psychological disorders such as depression, anxiety, and stress.

If a critical situation lasts for a longer period of time, people enter into one of two emotional states: catastrophizing or euphoria. Both are problematic.

Catastrophizing is dangerous because after all the stress you can only see a negative outcome and you lose all hope for a positive ending. You might feel paralyzed by the fear that your whole world will collapse. In regard to relationships, you might have thoughts such as, "If we split up, I'll never find someone like him or her again." In those cases, you need to widen your perspective and imagination to include the positive aspects of your situation and to reduce your stress level.

Euphoria is a more pleasant state of mind than catastrophizing, but in a critical situation it's no less dangerous. The problem is that in a temporary high mood you lose sight of the risks that still exist, and you don't make any effort to manage the situation. In a relationship crisis, this would sound like, "Hey, we had such a wonderful day.

Problem solved." In an extended period of stress, the hope for instantaneous healing is only human. But be careful. One positive sign doesn't mean that the crisis is over. Before you relax, you need to make sure that the roots of the critical situation really have been addressed.

The art of keeping your head in a crisis relies on neither catastrophizing nor becoming euphoric, as you risk becoming either paralyzed or passive while an increased readiness for action is needed. A certain amount of stress helps in these situations. It prompts you to ask pertinent questions and tackle the risk actively. It's very important to manage one's stress level and neither allow too much stress nor too little. The following suggestions might help:

- Is your situation critical and has it been like that for a while? What areas of your life are affected (health, relationship, income), and are there any existential risks?
- Observe your thoughts. Are you catastrophizing? You can recognize this if you hear yourself thinking, "It will go downhill anyway!" or "If that goes down the drain, it'll have catastrophic consequences and I won't be able to handle it" or "I can't do this, and if I don't manage it, they'll sack me and I'll never again find another job." You should also explore your thoughts to recognize whether your mind is overwhelmed by euphoria: "This is a good sign that the crisis is over" or "Yeah, I have an in-

vitation for an interview. I'm no longer unemployed!" It's a good idea to observe one's thoughts all the time and if you don't want to get lost in feelings in your day-to-day business, it's also a good idea to be conscious of your emotions. When you realize that in a critical situation you tend to either catastrophize or become euphoric, then name the experience but refrain from judging it. Say to yourself, "My thoughts are catastrophizing" or "These thoughts are euphoric." You could keep a thought diary and at the end of each day, take stock of what emotional states you experienced. But try not to label or judge your thoughts or find arguments for or against them.

– If you generally tend to catastrophize, it could be a sign of anxiety or depression that you should discuss with a doctor. If you only sporadically catastrophize, the following can help: lower your stress levels by exercising and using relaxation techniques, such as meditation. Perhaps take longer breaks or regularly do conscious breathing exercises. Widen your perceptions by consciously reflecting on the positive aspects and options in your situation. What is good at this very moment? What is not totally bad? Have I coped with something like this before? How did I do it? Do my friends see any possibilities of resolving the situation in a positive sense? Are there any solutions I haven't considered yet? Is it possible that the worst outcome of my situation is not as catastrophic as I imagine?

- If you are the euphoric type, you should ask yourself, while the situation is ongoing, "Is it possible that I have overestimated the tiny green shoots? Has the threat really passed? Are there any risks I should be prepared for?" Here is an example: you are urgently looking for a job and your financial situation is critical. If you get an invitation for an interview, you can be very happy, but don't become euphoric. Reflect on the fact that an interview isn't a job offer. Apply for other positions and enhance your prospects of a more secure financial future.
- Stress symptoms act as a smoke alarm. Don't consider stress an enemy you have to beat or remove. Often, stress symptoms are indicators that we need to change something in our situation or resolve the factors producing the stress in the first place. It can be counterproductive to simply reduce stress instead of rooting out the problem altogether. Just as with a beeping smoke alarm, we should find out where the smoke is coming from and then extinguish the fire, rather than just taking the batteries out. Do you know what sets off your alarms? Everyone's stress alarm is different—sleeping problems, headaches, heart and circulatory problems, heartburn, problems with concentration, dizziness, lack of motivation, irritations. Once you know your alarms and ac-

knowledge them, you are able to start searching for the origin and prevent a larger fire. Ask yourself, "What is my stress alarm telling me?" "What can I do to deal with the problem behind it?" It might be necessary to change your job or your working conditions instead of training yourself to endure the stress. You could probably prevent burnout by taking your stress symptoms seriously at an early stage and making fundamental improvements to your situation.

Self-efficacy—Leave the victim role behind and start being active.

In a crisis or in stressful times, it's very valuable to leave the feeling of hopelessness behind, and start trusting your own capabilities to handle the crisis and take action. The concept of so-called self-efficacy expectation comes from the Canadian psychologist Albert Bandura. He describes it as the subjective expectation of being able to handle a challenging situation at one's own speed. People who are confident in their capacity to deal with life tackle challenges more optimistically and actively and display more stamina than people who don't trust their own capacities very much. Eventually, people with high self-efficacy suffer less from depression, burnout symptoms, or pain. They manage traumatic situations better than people with less trust in their own capacities.

Self-efficacy starts developing in the first few months

of life. When babies realize that their parents come when they cry or that the rattle makes a sound when shaken, they learn that their actions have an impact. But adults can develop their self-efficacy relatively easily as well. You can easily introduce the following five self-efficacy steps into your life:

- Learn from your personal experiences. The more often you notice how your own actions can influence a situation or improve it, the more your trust in your own capabilities will grow. Try setting yourself small goals—a short run rather than a marathon—and allow yourself to be proud to have achieved something on your own steam. This will increase your motivation to face the next challenge.
- Look for a role model. It's best to settle on someone you trust, who has a similar character to you or is in a comparable life situation so you can identify better. Follow your role model in the sense of "If my friend manages to stop smoking, then I can do it too." A model set by someone else can easily be integrated in your day-to-day life.
- Allow yourself to be encouraged. Praise from family or friends can have a positive effect on your self-efficacy. Positive cheering and trust in you ("you can do it!") motivates action. If you complete a challenge, like passing an exam, it strengthens your own trust in your capabilities.

- Interpret your body's responses in a positive way. The way we interpret physical sensations has a strong influence on our self-efficacy. If you sweat before an exam, don't say "Oh, no, I'm so nervous. It's my fear of failure!" Instead think, "Great, my body is on full alert and ready to get going!"
- Help others. This is my personal tip for emergencies! The role of a helper is very rewarding, as you can do something meaningful in a bad situation and gain strength from it. You not only help others, but yourself, too.

Social support — Get stronger together

Social support has a positive effect on mental wellbeing and is the most evidenced psychological factor with an impact on physical health. People with a well-functioning social network suffer considerably fewer illnesses and mortal risks than socially isolated people. We can get different levels of support from our families, friends, and acquaintances, all of which help us manage difficult times or events. This includes emotional support like attention, comfort, or helpful conversations, but also the feeling of belonging and being backed. But practical support too, such as money or other donations, can mitigate an acutely critical situation. We also appreciate support such as the provision of helpful information or concrete pointers of where to find help. The knowledge of not being alone enhances our confidence to be able to cope with imminent challenges.

What can you actively do to benefit from social support when in need?

- Widen your social network. Invest in stable relationships with other people. Building up trust and mutual appreciation takes time. You should start early to work on your relationships and not only when you need help. A good relationship is based on mutual give and take. It's better to give from the heart and without any expectation of a return.
- Look for help. Are you one of those people who in times of need retreats into their shell and tries to manage on their own? Then you should change this for the sake of your health. Get help, whether from your friends or colleagues. This will protect your own resources and increase your chances of success.
- Real friends give real help. Friends in need aren't always the easiest people, but they are those who are serious about you. They have open and honest conversations with you and do so for your sake and without pity. Real friends go out of their way to help you in your need and try to give you strength by helping you to help yourself.

Fitness — Get stronger physically and mentally "A healthy mind in a healthy body."

This proverb, from the Roman poet Juvenal, shows how

closely physical and mental fitness are connected. Mental attitude has a great impact on physical fitness. This means that we have to overcome our inner sloth and get up from the sofa to exercise—to eat fruit instead of potato chips. Never let up! But how do we do that? I will give you three suggestions that help me to keep fit in everyday life.

- Don't try to achieve too much. Don't fall prey to a new year's resolution and ask too much of yourself with plans that are too ambitious, and then throw in the towel in disappointment. Rather, move step by step in the right direction and stay on the ball. Make a plan that includes personal fitness goals and activities you want to do, such as "walk around the block during my lunch break," "eat more greens," "take an alcohol-free day." Stick the plan to your bathroom mirror. Every night, tick off items you have managed that day and complete the list before you add more. This strategy has an advantage over a new year's resolution—it starts with easy steps, it charts your successes, and you get motivated and can then integrate further tasks into your daily routine.
- Remember the basics of good health and follow them. There are hundreds of strict diets and hardcore fitness programs that are thrown at us as the solution to all physical problems. In most cases, your health program ends up being a mix of different

rules that you were first told by your grandmother—eat well, drink enough, take fresh air on a regular basis, relax regularly, get enough sleep, do without toxic substances such as cigarettes or alcohol. My personal tip: just observe all the basic rules for keeping healthy rather than focusing all your energy on one element while neglecting others.
– Be disciplined. To overcome your inner sloth, you need discipline. You can train for that by having a cold shower every morning, for example. That will take you out of your comfort zone and increase your energy level.

I'm sure that right now you already know and do many of these things. You are already on the right path to cope with your challenges. Maybe at this very moment you are in a difficult situation and can introduce one or two of these suggestions into your life. The earlier you increase your own resources, the more you can rely on them in difficult times. But don't try to achieve too much at one time. Rather, choose one or two items, start introducing them today and then increase them—step by step.

You certainly will have coped with some crises in your life before. To get through a crisis with strength and afterwards get up again is worth a lot. But in my view, a crisis is not just a hurdle to get over, but a step through which we can grow to better ourselves. Negative experiences contain potential for positive development. I only recognized this quite late, but have since made use of it. Here are some suggestions for how to consciously grow in a crisis. In my experience, the following three steps play an important role:

1. Acknowledge a crisis.
2. Look for opportunities.
3. Dare to make changes.

Acknowledge a Crisis

The first, most difficult and important step toward growing through a crisis is to admit to oneself that things can't go on as they are. Too often we cling to the familiarity of the past. But we can only tackle something new when we let go of some old things. That's why it's important to acknowledge the irreversibility of some situations and to grieve what we have lost—for example a relationship, a job, a loved one, or an aspect of our health. The following steps might be helpful:

– Stop and take stock of your situation. Maybe your umpteenth relationship has failed because of the same issue, or at work you ended up burning out because of the same stress as before. Perhaps a sudden event, like an accident, has turned your life upside down. That is all terrible. But try to look at your *actual* situation as soon as the first shock has subsided.

- Grieve. Treat yourself with the same consideration as you would treat a friend. Allow yourself to feel the pain and a sense of helplessness. Everyone grieves in their own way and in their own time. When you have lost a loved one, professional help can be valuable in the grieving process.
- Accept that things cannot go on as before. Don't gloss over your situation, saying things like, "My relationship is over? Well, I'll start another one." You will miss the chance to learn from your experience and you will repeat the mistakes.
- Don't blame yourself. Thoughts like, "If only …" or "If that hadn't happened …" or "Why me?" in the long run rob you of the energy you need to cope with the crisis and to transform it. Acknowledge that you can't turn the clock back.
- Take the crisis as a challenge and an invitation to change. Accept that it is time to look for new paths and to start walking. Focus your energy forward.

Look for Opportunities

"A crisis is an opportunity." They already knew this in ancient China and Greece. But these opportunities have to be taken, and it doesn't work when you simply carry on falling over and then get up again, dust yourself off and walk on, like a tumbler toy. That process puts you back on the carousel of crises again, and you repeat the same experience. Taking advantage of the opportunity for change, you can choose a new path and get off that not so merry merry-go-round. To do that, it's useful to look for opportunities from your own past experiences. Even if you have been thrown off course only once, and maybe by accident, it's worthwhile to look for opportunities of how to make the most of the situation. Ask yourself some of the following questions:

- What can I learn from the crisis? Have I experienced something similar before? If yes, why? Where is the connection? For example, have I been burnt out before? Were the demands on me the same? Did the same kinds of people stress me out? What does it have to do with me? What can I learn about me from this situation?
- Am I part of the problem? That would be good, because then I can be part of the solution as well. It's uncomfortable when you realize that you play a part in a failure. But at the same time, this insight brings relief. You are not a victim anymore, hopelessly exposed to circumstances. Now there is an opportunity to take your fate into your own hands by changing something about yourself.
- What can I change to make my life better? Is it

about learning to set clearer boundaries and to say *no* every now and then? Or do I have to care about my health more? Can I learn to deal with money better to avoid another bankruptcy?

– What opportunities come from my new situation? What have I always dreamed of? What makes my eyes light up? Paint a picture of your desired future. Did I always want to change my job and after this reorganization now have the chance to do it? Do I take the failure of my relationship as a starting point to improve myself in a self-development seminar or workshop? Didn't I always want to get involved with people more and can now make use of my own experience and do bereavement work? Hadn't I always wanted to run a sheep farm in Australia and can do this now, because I don't have any work or personal commitments?

Dare to Change

"Difficult times allow us to develop determination and strength." (Dalai Lama)

People often find the courage to change when they think they have nothing to lose. Why would you start on the risky and arduous path toward self-employment when you have a secure job? Why would you spend time on self-development when really everything is all right? A crisis doesn't only force us to make changes, but it might make it easier to try something new. Life is upside down anyway. But after a serious blow, the comfort zone is attractive, and people love returning to it.

Stress at work is forgotten after a while; after a breakup, another relationship opportunity can quickly arise; bankruptcy can be avoided by a generous gift from relatives. Why then change something fundamental in your life? In order to make use of the opportunities for change, you have to convert them into determination and truly dare to seize them. The following steps will help you toward it:

- Use the momentum of the crisis to make changes! Try to view the blow as a hint from fate to take you out of your comfort zone into a zone in which you can grow. You possibly have nothing to lose right now and can dare something that you would never have dreamed of before. Do something you've never dared to do before or were possibly too lazy for.
- Try out a new a path! Don't go on like before! Don't return blindly to old relationships or jobs.
- Stick it out! Trust your inner voice and your vision of the future. You might find that not everyone around you will support it. Not everyone will like that you are changing. Some might even want to persuade you back to the old role. "Before, you never said *no* when I asked you for something." Perhaps your changes even challenge certain social conven-

tions. "You can't simply go off and run a sheep farm in Australia! That's a foolish dream!"

- Don't fall back into old habits. Maybe you end up saying *yes* to please someone, even though you had decided to maintain better boundaries and say *no* when you don't feel like doing something. It's not bad to just do a lap of honor with your old habits, but it's important that you recognize it and allow it to remind you of your resolution. Practice makes perfect. The main thing is that you don't fall back into the old patterns; otherwise, you might have to do another round on the crisis carousel.
- Be proud of your courage and be gentle with yourself when it doesn't work out perfectly straightaway. Toddlers are great role models. They fall over hundreds of times a day when they are learning to walk.

Hopefully, you have found some of the suggestions helpful for how to grow from the major events in your life. It would be great if you'd feel encouraged to actively search for opportunities and turn your life for the better by making courageous changes—or at least make the best of your situation. It is the difficult phases in life from which you gain the impulse for a new beginning or to take another direction.

Luckily, there aren't only turbulent phases in a life. There is always a calm after the storm and long phases when life goes on in an uneventful way. It's a good idea to consciously enjoy the easy-going times. Do you have moments when you love your life just as it is so much that you would like to remember it forever? And have you experienced the terror of all that might happen in the future that could turn your life upside down? What if my wonderful relationship doesn't last after all? What if my company goes bust or I have a serious health problem? How would I deal with that? Would I be able to cope?

From my own experience, I know that we can prepare ourselves actively for future challenges. It's not only current or recent crises that can give us strength. We can also actively access the creative potential of a years-old crisis and cultivate a relaxed attitude toward the future. The easy and happy phases of life are particularly well suited for these explorations. It's then that we have enough time and energy.

We can't always prevent a crisis, but we can steel ourselves for one. We can often find the necessary armor in our own treasure trove of experiences, but it is often buried deeply in our past. We have forgotten what crises we have already mastered, and particularly, how we did it. We can retrieve this treasure trove of experiences by consciously reflecting on our past life. My personal treasure of life experiences has made it possible for me not only to cope with my most recent crisis, but also to turn it into an opportunity in the best possible sense.

Retrieve Your Treasure Trove of Life Experiences

People generally get more relaxed with age and don't allow themselves to be thrown off track easily. If, for example, a new boss or a reorganization is announced at work, it's especially the younger colleagues who worry most. "Oh, what will that mean?" On the whole, senior colleagues react with more serenity. "It's not the end of the world." Why? It's because they probably have experienced a similar situation and survived it. Scientific studies prove that people who have experienced three or four life crises are particularly resilient and have a high level of mental resistance (Kalisch).

Life experience is a true treasure trove, particularly in difficult times. But it is not only important what we have experienced, but how we did it and processed it. Unfortunately, with most people, the treasure trove of life experiences is deeply buried. In many cultures, a personal crisis is a trigger for shame and therefore rather repressed or forgotten.

No matter how old you are, it makes a big difference when you consciously utilize your past experiences rather than leaving them untapped. Stop regretting past mistakes and crises, and begin to actively learn from them. After all, you have survived it once and cannot change it anymore. But you can consciously learn from those experiences and grow with them. You can also make sense of your past.

Before you go on a journey into your past, consider this warning: if you have experienced serious and traumatic problems, you may rediscover them, and it's better to have the support of a therapist. Otherwise, you can start now:

- Find a quiet place where you can begin your reflections, pen and paper at hand. Close your eyes for a moment and take some deep breaths.
- Before you go on your journey into the past, you should fortify yourself mentally. The more confidence you have in your own strengths, the easier it will be to look back on the more difficult chapters in your life. Be aware of your own strengths. You can support your explorations by making a list. Write down the letters A to Z on a piece of paper from top to bottom. Then take five minutes and brainstorm what strengths you can think of, one for each letter. A for being attentive … H as in humor, etc. The order doesn't matter. You don't have to find a strength for all the letters. This is about quick activation of your inner resources.
- Find your treasure trove of life experiences. Ask yourself, what difficulties have I overcome in my life, how often have I fallen down and still gotten up again afterwards? What kind of successes and achievements arose from those defeats? For example, has a previous breakup made it possible for you to now sustain a happy relationship? Did a dismissal

make it easier to make a long-desired job change? Try to find as many as possible of your critical life experiences and watersheds. It might feel peculiar at first because we normally polish our résumés instead of focusing on the low points. Perhaps you could go through your résumé year by year and reflect on the most important personal and professional events. Looking at old photos and diaries can enhance this search. Dealing with the past isn't always easy. For that reason, make yourself aware that you have managed to overcome all this! Be proud! You are a resilient person!

- Retrieve your treasure trove of life experiences. Go through the critical watersheds in your life one by one and ask yourself, how did I cope with this challenge? Was it through motivating conversations with friends? Inspiration from a role model? Prayers or maybe writing down my thoughts? What positive changes have arisen from this event? What am I proud of? Write down all your thoughts on a piece of paper and make a list of all your resources. Count your own skills and positive characteristics such as perseverance and humor, but also external resources like a stable social network. Have another look at the initial list of your strengths. Ideally, you could ask a trusted person to give you honest feedback about what strengths and weaknesses they perceive in you. A presumed weakness can turn out to be a valuable resource if you give it a second look. Egotism, for example, could also be interpreted as the capacity to look after yourself. That can be a helpful resource in a difficult situation.

- At the end of this reflection, you should have a clear picture of the positive aspects of your past negative experiences. You have made yourself aware of what adversities you have mastered so far and what resources have helped you to do it. Now you will find it easier to rely on your inner strength and look into the future with more serenity.
- Increase your treasure trove of life experiences. Enjoy the calm and untroubled phases in your life that you have experienced. It's good to take a deep breath and recharge, especially after a stormy period. But don't stay too long in the comfort zone. Look proactively for new challenges through which you can grow. Resilience is like a muscle you build up by training, but it gets flabby again without exercise. Keep moving and leave your comfort zone often. Leave the conveyor belt of everyday life and do things you have never done before or never dared to do, such as a cross-country run. Develop your self-awareness by going to a personal development workshop. Give your relationship a new impulse by proactively facing uncomfortable issues. Don't get too cozy in your job, but look for new challenges. Realize the lifetime dream you have been postponing for

years; possibly go traveling or change careers. There are many possibilities for staying active and increasing the treasure trove of life experiences. Of course, it's not easy to beat the inner sloth time and again and change something in your life when it's so cozy right now. But if you stop changing, sooner or later a crisis will force you into it. Keep moving and get fit for the future!

- Walk through life with strength and you'll grow even stronger during the difficult times. If you have come up with some new ideas for your life, it's best to take the first steps today.

ACKNOWLEDGEMENTS

This book is the result of a process of resilience in motion.

Writing it was made possible by the support from my social and professional environment.

Most of all I want to thank my wife and my children for their loving support and their flexibility even when there was another extra shift to do.

I want to thank my parents and my brother with all my heart for their support and trust in this biographical reappraisal. It also tells part of their own stories.

To Jürgen Diessl of Econ Verlag, I owe gratitude for his extraordinary trust and involvement in my journey. He has made it possible to fulfill the dream of a lifetime. My thanks go to my editor, Dr. Annalisa Viviani, for her competent, unshakeable, clear, and empathetic way of enhancing my manuscript—and me.

I also want to thank all the people who have helped me with recommendations, professional advice, contributions, valuable feedback, successful cover shoots and heartfelt encouragement to realize the project, particularly Emanuel Koch, Susanne Kreuzer, Alexa Lorenz, Sarah Mainka, Sebastian Mauritz, Palma Müller-Scherf, Ulrike Scheuermann, Lars Schulze Kossack, Stefan Schwidder, Martin Spütz, Michael Thenner, Lukas Wagner, and Stephanie Wolff.

And lastly, I want to thank the many encouraging and challenging encounters that inspired me to write this book and allowed me to grow through it.

BIBLIOGRAPHY

Amman, G. / Egger, A.: *Micro-Inputs Resilienz – Lebendige Modelle, Interventionen und Visualisierungshilfen für das Resilienz-Coaching und-Training.* Bonn 2017.

Bengel, J. / Lyssenko, L.: *Resilienz und psychologische Schutzfaktoren im Erwachsenenalter – Stand der Forschung zu psychologischen Schutzfaktoren von Gesundheit im Erwachsenenalter.* Bundeszentrale für gesundheitliche Aufklärung (Hg.). Köln 2012.

Berndt, C: *Resilienz – Das Geheimnis der psychischen Widerstandskraft – Was uns stark macht gegen Stress, Depression und Burn-out.* München 2015.

Böhme, Rebecca: *Resilienz.* München 2019.

Collins, J: *Der Weg zu den Besten: Die sieben Management-Prinzipien für dauerhaften Unternehmenserfolg.* Frankfurt a. M. 2003.

Cullberg, J: *Krise als Entwicklungschance.* Gießen 2008.

Daigeler, T. / Krüger, W.: *Führen.* München 2012.

Dluzniewski, J: *Das Essenz-Modell – Die eigene Urwunde erkennen und die wahre Lebensaufgabe entdecken.* Berlin 2020.

Heller, J. (Hg.): *Resilienz für die VUCA-Welt – Individuelle und organisationale Resilienz entwickeln.* Wiesbaden 2018.

Kalisch, R.: *Der resiliente Mensch – Wie wir Krisen erleben und bewältigen.* Berlin 2017.

Kaluza, G.: *Stressbewältigung – Trainingsmanual zur psychologischen Gesundheitsförderung.* Berlin 2018.

Lepore, S. F. / Evans, G. W.: »Coping with multiple stressors in the environment«, in: Zeidner, M., Endler, N. S. (Hg.): *Handbook of coping: Theory, research, applications,* Oxford 1996, S. 350–377.

Masten, A.: *Resilienz: Modelle, Fakten und Neurobiologie – Das ganz normale Wunder entschlüsselt.* Paderborn 2016.

Mauritz, S: *Immun gegen Probleme, Stress und Krisen – Wie unser Leben gelingen kann.* Offenbach 2019.

Ders.: *Wenn schon Burn-out, dann richtig – 10 + Tipps für den totalen Burn-out.* Göttingen 2013.

Popow, Heinrich: https://www.spiegel.de/sport/sonst/paralympics-2012-heinrich-popow-will-gold-ueber-100-meter-a-853563.html

Schmidt, G. / Dollinger, A. / Müller-Kalthoff, B. (Hg.): *Gut beraten in der Krise – Konzepte und Werkzeuge für ganz alltägliche Ausnahmesituationen.* Bonn 2019.

TK-Stressstudie 2016, *Entspann dich, Deutschland,* https://www.tk.de/resource/blob/2026630/9154e4c71766c410dc859916aa798217/tk-stressstudie-2016-data.pdf

Tuckman, B. W. / Jensen, M. A.: »Stages of small-group development revisited, in: *Group and Organization Stu-*

dies 1977, https://pdfs.semanticscholar.org/82ce/5d6862e726c9221104fe67b0e3c8fe890b9a.pdf

Waldbaden: https://www.zeit.de/zeit-wissen/2018/03/waldbaden-natur-heilung-gesundheit-japan/seite-2

Wellensiek, S.: *Handbuch Resilienz-Training: Widerstandskraft und Flexibilität für Unternehmen und Mitarbeiter.* Weinheim 2011.

Welter-Enderlin, R. / Hildenbrand, B. (Hg.): *Resilienz – Gedeihen trotz widriger Umstände.* Heidelberg 2008.